If Knowledge is Power,
You are about to become a Genius.

IMPORTANT CAUTION — PLEASE READ THIS!

No Portion of Delilah Power! is intended as medical advice and in no way excludes the necessity of diagnosis and/or treatment from a health professional. Any application of treatments set forth in any part of this book is strictly at the reader's discretion and neither the author nor publisher assumes any responsibility or liability therefore. The intent of this book is solely for entertainment purposes. Readers are strongly cautioned to consult with a physician or other health-care professional before engaging in the exercises described in this book and to adapt the exercises in the book to meet the reader's special needs and limitations.

This book is based on information from sources believed to be reliable and an effort has been made to make the book as complete and accurate as possible based on information available as of the printing date, but its accuracy cannot be guaranteed. Despite the best efforts of author and publisher, the book may contain mistakes and the reader should use the book only as a general guide and not as the ultimate source of information about the subject of the book. The book is not intended to reprint all of the information available to the author or publisher on the subject, but rather to simplify, complement and supplement other available sources. The reader is therefore encouraged to read all available material and to learn as much as possible about the subject. Some of these materials may be listed as RELATED RESOURCES elsewhere in the book. Materials listed as related resources are noted for their relevance to the subjects discussed and not as an endorsement of any product or service.

This book may contain information from, and unedited portions of anonymous surveys and interviews. The participants were asked to express their views candidly. Such views printed in this book are not necessarily those of the author or publisher.

Any and all names used in case illustrations are fictitious and represent a compilation of various anonymous interviews held both live and through printed questionnaires. Such names are not intended to, nor do they represent any person living or dead. In addition, any characters described are imaginary and any resemblance to actual persons, living or dead, is purely coincidental.

This book is sold without warranties of any kind, express or implied, and the publisher and author disclaim any liability, loss or damage caused by the contents of this book.

If you do not wish to be bound by the foregoing cautions and conditions, you may return this book directly to the publisher for a full refund.

Delilah Power!

Tannis Blackman

Delilah Power!
The Millennium Edition

Tannis Blackman

© 1997, 2000 by Tannis Blackman
First Printing 1997
Second Printing 2000, revised
Book design and illustrations by G. Clark
Cover illustration by Cleopatra

Published by:

Swing Street
Box #846, Cathedral Station
New York, NY 10025-0846 USA

Library of Congress Catalog Card Number: 99-76930

ISBN: 0-9652540-4-6 11.95

Swing Street Books can be purchased at special rates when ordered in large quantities by corporations, organizations or groups, for educational use, fund raising and sales promotions. Special messages, excerpts and imprints can be produced to your specifications. For more information, contact the Special Sales Manager at the address listed above. Please indicate how you intend to use the books (e.g., resale, premiums, etc.).

Prepared with the support and assistance of Fauve, Inc.

Printed in The United States of America

This book is dedicated to every woman of color who holds *Delilah Power!* in her hands for she undoubtedly reads in search of enlightenment. This book is also dedicated to my best friend Marcelle, whose courage in the face of adversity has been my inspiration.

Acknowledgements

A Book has no value without a reader. To my readers: Thank you for allowing me to express my ideas and share what I've learned with you. I hope this book proves helpful and you enjoy reading it as much as I've enjoyed writing it. We're all in this together. Why not lift each other up?

To the friends and associates who have offered their unending support to me during this project: Thank you. No need to mention any names. You all know who you are and there's much love for ya!

Thanks to my family: I love you more than anything. Yea, we have our differences sometimes, but what would life be without a little drama? When the stuff hits the fan, you are the ones I automatically turn to. And you have never let me down. Thanks for always being there for me.

Special thanks to my mother, whom I love dearly and without whom, I would not exist. You have been and will always be my backbone, my life's blood, my anchor and my foundation. Your constant support, selfless caring and undying faith are what lifted our family from the bottom. Without you, I could not have grown into the person that I am. You continually inspire me and I can only hope to one day become half the woman you naturally are. I want you to be as proud of me as I am of you. You're the best!

Last but not least, I wish to give complete and total thanks to the Universal Spirit, the omnipresent force recognized by all and revered with so many names. I know that I am blessed and so I act with divine guidance. I will keep striving to fulfill my ultimate purpose and not falter. The path you've chosen for me is often rough and confusing, but I know there is reward at the end. I know that you love me and love must sometimes be tough. I surrender my life to you without fear, for my life is and will always be in your caring hands.

Delilah Power!

Table of Contents

Part Three
Practica

Part Four
Completion

Introduction

Delilah Power! is for every woman in the world who is out there, searching for something. Although each woman's quest may vary, the rewards harvested by reading this book remain the same. Every woman has some degree of Delilah in her. And every woman can benefit greatly from *Delilah Power!*

Imagine yourself standing in front of a gold mine and all you need do to achieve wealth is dig. This book aims to provide you with a wealth of information and help you live your life at your optimal physical, mental and spiritual capacity. *Delilah Power!* is for women of color who strive for inner and outer cultivation.

In the new millennium, there will be two categories of women: those with the knowledge and those without. Resources for Black women are often limited and it can be difficult for us to obtain specific types of information. When I came up with the idea for *Delilah Power!*, I asked myself what kind of knowledge I would like to gain from a self-help book and what would keep me interested in its content. For me, learning has to be *fun*.

I've attempted then, to provide you with a reference source that is both entertaining and enlightening. There were a number of people and entities I had to consult with to complete this project: from government agencies to business professionals, medical personnel and endless websites, a lawyer, an accountant, a mechanic, cosmetologist, fashion designer, clairvoyant and so on. Ultimately, writing *Delilah Power!* has been a blessing for me, because I've learned so much in the process. And it has been fun!

Delilah Power! is divided into four complete sections. The first two sections, *Exotica* and *Erotica*, focus on love, sex and self-exploration. *Practica* and *Completion* address the trials and tribulations of everyday living, as well as information and skills you need to maximize your health and increase your prosperity.

If reading *Delilah Power!* motivates you in any way, increases your awareness and spirituality or helps you to improve your relationships with men, prompts you to become more independent or conduct your personal business more efficiently, makes sex more enjoyable or inspires you to pass the knowledge on, then I've achieved my goal. Without each other, we have nothing. Each one teach one and we all prosper!

Why Delilah?

One night, I was having a friendly debate with a male friend, the topic was men and women in relationships. My friend insisted that women are inherently devious, constantly aiming to seduce innocent men for their own fiendish purposes. He cited Cleopatra, queen of Egypt, Mata Hari, celebrated spy and Delilah from the Samson and Delilah legend to support his argument. There were others he mentioned, including a woman who reportedly seduced a president and nearly cost him his job, but the first three, particularly Delilah, remained uppermost in my mind.

I knew enough about Samson and Delilah to know it was a Biblical story from the Old Testament. My friend was on an ignorance crusade, so I asked him to tell me what he knew about the legend. According to him, the premise was very simple: strong man with long hair and incredible strength meets irresistible woman with clippers and penis envy. Samson has instinctive fear of Delilah and avoids her like "an anal probe." So, Delilah goes about her task of finding Samson's weakness with the tenacity of a bee (it turns out Samson's powers come directly from his hair), seducing him, psyching him out and even resorting to murder to get to the core of his amazing strength. Delilah's wicked beauty is what finally does Samson in. She wastes no time in shaving him down, leaving him bald-headed, weak, and totally disgusted. My friend's version of the story ends with

Samson blind and pushing boulders for the rest of his life, while Delilah's realizing her mistake and wishing she could have her old man back.

After staring at this guy for a while with my mouth open, then telling him what I knew of the real story, I tried to understand his perceptions. I conceded some analysts might say Samson's hair was symbolic, perhaps a phallic symbol, representative of the penis. In such a case, the story would illustrate that man (Samson) was castrated by woman (Delilah) and man has much to consider when he sees phenomenal breasts and buns coming his way. I had to point out though that the average woman doesn't want to "castrate" her man. Chances are she loves, wants and needs every bit of him, especially his "penis". At the end of the debate, my friend and I finally managed to agree on something: Delilah was a powerful woman who fought for what she believed in. And it didn't take long for me to name this book *Delilah Power!*

So, who is Delilah in this day and age? Delilah is a conqueror! She conquers all because she is all woman: pure female with nothing to prove, except to herself and everything to gain. She draws her strength from within, using positive means and knowledge to attain her every desire. She has that special thing called *Delilah Power!* You now hold the power in your hands. With this book, *Delilah Power!* is yours and all you'll ever need!

Please note *Delilah Power!* bears no relation whatsoever to the Samson and Delilah story or the Old Testament. In addition, this book in no way intends to ridicule or disrespect the religious beliefs of others. To learn more about the legend of Samson and Delilah, consult the Old Testament.

A last comment on the penis envy theory: sure, some men deserve to be "cut down" to size, but we'll leave that to the *playa haters*. Here, for the purposes of this book, girls just wanna have FUN! (and gain a wealth of knowledge, of course!)

Creating Your Personal Pages...

For many people, putting one's thoughts, experiences and emotions on paper can be helpful. Throughout this book, you will find pages devoted just to you, for your own personal thoughts and feelings. Should you decide to explore what these pages have to offer, they will most likely reflect a very intimate part of you, the part that is learning, growing, changing and ultimately becoming more powerful. It is suggested you use your pages to write down whatever perceptions you have, whether concerning a disturbing dream you remember, an emotional episode, general thoughts, or a letter you may never want anyone else to see. Although some topics are suggested, you can and should write about whatever you feel at the moment. Once you finish reading this book, you will be able to review your personal pages and combine them into a complete chapter that is yours and yours alone. And it may very well become one of your most prized possessions.

At first, you may find it difficult to begin the writing process, especially if you've never kept a journal or diary. Journal keeping does not come easily for everyone. Do not force yourself. However, if you ever find yourself wanting to make a note of an item you read, or you have a revelation, or suddenly form an opinion of something, why not use the spaces provided? Once your pen touches the paper, it may begin to move by its own accord and before you know it, you will have completed a page upon which you can proudly reflect.

In the future, you may refer to your personal pages for insight and information that will prove useful in your quest to accomplish your goals. As the expression goes, hindsight is 20/20. A parting word of advice: like any other intimate item, personal pages should be kept safe from prying eyes.

The First Page of my Personal Chapter

Writing the first page can be the most difficult. Suggestions: What do I want to accomplish by reading this book? What questions will I seek to answer? How do I feel about change and growth? How am I feeling about myself right now?

_____

_____

_____

_____

_____

_____

_____

_____

_____

_____

_____

_____

_____

_____

This is YOUR personal page. Write on! ✎ *More space on the reverse...*

Part One

Exotica

When Heaven and Earth
Become One...

From Hair to Lair
Perfecting the Art of Seduction

Imagine yourself as an Egyptian queen. You languish on your royal throne, enjoying the warm African breeze against your skin, listening to the peaceful waters of the Nile. You're surrounded by magnificent men: powerful eunuchs, black and smooth and glossy as crude oil, each at your imperial command. Your body is draped with fine linen and silk, the jewelry adorning you is hand-forged from solid gold. Your pampered feet are intricately dyed with henna and your tresses, elaborately woven with jewels. You spend your days and nights in elegant splendor, waited upon by your subjects and admired. You captivate men. The king may reign, but *you* rule. You're considered the most fascinating woman of all, because you have a special power. You are the ultimate seductress.

When the king visits your chamber, he does so with the anxious anticipation of being pleased and pleased well. You know better than any woman how to excite him: how to look, smell, move and act. You're his mate and you make him feel like a real man. When you greet your king, scented with exotic perfumes, skin softened with luscious oils and oozing sensuality, the man loses his royal mind. Unchained desire takes control and destroys his will. He grabs you in his massive arms, kisses you passionately and thrusts himself into you, bringing you to orgasm as only a king possibly could.

This is what making love to a man can be like when you use *Delilah Power!* to your advantage. To heighten your sexual pleasure (and his), you need to perfect the art of seduction and make a commitment to pampering yourself. This is what *From Hair to Lair* is all about.

From the moment you catch a man's eye, you are in a position to win his heart. A simple look, the right look, can set the stage for making him yours forever. In this chapter, you'll master flirtation, provocative ways to capture a male's attention. Your skills will be cultivated with lessons on irresistible body language, visual contact and using your voice as an incredible enticement ploy. You will also become skilled in the power of illusion: fully aware of how the right cosmetics, clothes and hairstyle can evoke whatever sentiment you desire. You're a hardworking woman. Now, it's playtime! Tempt him, tease him, intrigue him, or fill him with longing. The choice and luxury are yours!

Seduction is a woman's specialty because she is far more intuitive, quick-witted and skillful than a man. There is an old saying: sex is an act of nature, but it makes a man a fool. It takes away his money and wears out his tool. Seduction can keep your sex life fresh and prevent boredom. A man who is intrigued by his woman remains interested. You can intrigue a man both in and out of bed, knowing the greatest seduction of all involves his *mind*. Seduction is healthy for both of you because you feel desirable and his ego is satisfied.

Seducing a New Man

Seducing a new man is fairly easy. Keeping him is the challenging part. When it comes to seduction, there is one basic rule: the way you *get* a man is the way you'll have to *keep* him. If you use sex as your main bait, sex will be your only bargaining chip. If you seduce a man with lies, you'll have to continue telling lies to keep him interested. If however you reveal the best part of yourself and appeal to the man's intellect, your relationship will have more staying power.

Step 1: When you meet a new man, your attitude and manner will determine whether or not he will approach you. Although men are normally expected to pursue, many of them hesitate when they *really* like a woman. If a man interests you and you appear happy, full of life and receptive, you increase the chances he'll approach you. Keep in mind however, some men act disinterested when they are in fact, *very* interested. The disinterest is a shield they use to cover their fear and shyness and to protect themselves against possible rejection.

If you suspect a man may be interested, nothing works better than a smile to put him at ease and let him know you're approachable. As they say, a smile is the second best thing you can do with your lips! When his eyes meet yours, give him a sincere smile which proclaims: "I think you're someone I'd like to meet. Why not come over and get to know me?" Once you've gotten him into your space, move to step 2: flirtation.

Step 2: Flirtation is your way of letting a man know you recognize and appreciate his masculinity. We'll begin first with a study of the voice and move to what most men perceive as irresistible body language.

The Voice

Your voice can be an amazing enticement. You can make a man listen to you for hours if you learn to use your voice correctly. Your voice should be melodic, like a beautiful piece of music that soothes and stimulates him, the sound if it emerging from your throat and not your nose. You can use your seductive voice on the phone, when making love, or any other time you want a male to be enraptured.

Men love women who exude femininity. Therefore, when you seduce a man, speak softly. Always sound a touch out of breath and occasionally sigh as though you are hopelessly in love. This may sound silly, but it works! Don't overdo it by attempting to sound like a 900#. Also avoid profanity. You want to be sexy without being overtly sexual. The trick is to make him wonder if you sound that way because you're turned on by him, or just because you sound so *amazing*.

You can practice softening your voice by making a deep humming sound and focusing on the tonal quality.

Next, try saying a few words with the same quality and gradually move to sentences. Allow inflections in your voice to come naturally while maintaining the same soft quality. You don't want your voice to sound mechanical or monotone. Practice your breathing. Breath slowly and rhythmically and focus on relaxing. You'll know you've mastered the technique when you try it on a man and he keeps remarking on you how great you sound.

Body language

Body language is non-verbal communication, an unspoken medium to convey what you want and how you're feeling. Irresistible body language is that which invites a man to come closer:

- ♥ Leaning near him so that he can feel your aura and smell you.
- ♥ Smiling at him demurely as he flirts with you.
- ♥ Gazing at him admiringly as he talks and moves.
- ♥ Touching him occasionally on the arm, shoulder or back as you're speaking.
- ♥ Allowing him to touch you in return, as long as it's in a non-assuming and appropriate way.
- ♥ Looking up at him as though awed by his size and masculinity.
- ♥ Hanging on his every word, as if what he says is the most important thing in the world.

In short, playing the feminine role so that he can fully express his maleness. All of these things will make a man feel validated. As his confidence grows, he'll reveal more of himself to you. With each encounter, he'll be eager to see more of you. Use your intuition to discover what the man finds pleasing.

A note about touching: some men are not comfortable when strange women touch them. If you touch a male and he recoils, don't do it again. Give him time to get used to you. If you touch him and he leans into you or touches you back, you know he's comfortable with the contact. Keep in mind that, by touching a man, you're also giving him non-verbal permission to touch *you.*

The Integumentary System: Hair, Skin and Nails

Contrary to what some Sisters believe, hair doesn't have to be long in order to be sexy. What turns a man on the most is hair that's clean, sweet-smelling and well-groomed. Long or short, relaxed or natural, your hair can be very seductive. Use it to your advantage!

Healthy hair is glossy, resilient and sexy. A good diet will help your hair maintain those qualities. You should also trim your ends every six to eight weeks. This helps to avoid split ends and excessive breakage. In order to keep your scalp smelling clean, wash your hair at least once a week. Don't apply too much grease or pomade, because they attract dirt and can make your scalp feel itchy. If you have dandruff, use a dandruff shampoo regularly and/or see a dermatologist.

If your face and neck are heavy, you may do well to sweep hair up for your seduction, or wear a style off the shoulders and close to the face. This elongates your neck and makes you appear slimmer and taller. Short cuts also look great on voluptuous women. If your face is thin, you can flesh it out by wearing a fuller style or cut. Curls also add bulk to your face and are very sexy.

Pubic hair is another consideration. Most women address the hair atop their heads, forgetting the hair men come face-to-face with. Entice him into licking you the right way by making the kitty more appetizing. When a man performs oral sex on you, he will truly appreciate a sweet-smelling pubic mound. Keep hairs closely cropped to minimize odor. Some women train and condition pubic hairs with small amount of leave-in conditioner after each shower, afterwards smoothing the hairs downward with a fine-toothed comb or soft brush. This reportedly produces lovely results.

If you scent the pubic mound, do so in moderation. Men like a whiff of fragrance, but they also want to smell the real you, as long as you're clean. A tip from one seductress: Dab pure vanilla extract. Men love it.

The Skin

The skin is the body's largest organ. Clear, soft skin reflects good health and is immensely appealing. To keep your skin looking seductive, drink plenty of water and eat a healthy diet. You can prevent acne by washing your skin daily and resisting the urge to pick. If you have severe acne, speak with your doctor. You may have an allergy to a particular food, need internal cleansing, or prescription medication.

Exercise and physical exertion are beneficial for skin because they increase circulation and cause sweating. When you sweat, toxins and impurities are released from your body through your pores. After exercising, wash or rinse your face thoroughly to remove dirt and prevent clogged pores.

Steaming your face is a great way to improve skin condition. All you need is a large pot of water and a towel. Bring water to a boil. Remove pot from heat. Hold the towel over your head like a tent and lean over the pot to capture the vapors. Within a minute or two, your face will be sweating profusely. Immediately follow up with a clay mask or mud pack, wash your face and splash it with cold water. Steam your face whenever it needs a good cleansing (once a week to once a month).

As women of color, we're gifted. The melanin which gives our skin its beautiful color also affords us some protection against the sun's harmful rays. As a general rule, the darker you are, the more protection you have.

This doesn't mean however, that you can't develop certain forms of skin cancer, or suffer from sunburn.

While sunburn is caused by UVB rays, wrinkling and certain forms of skin cancer are caused by UVA radiation. It's a good idea to use a lotion or cream with both UVA and UVB protection daily to help preserve your skin's youthful appearance. Always use a gentle, upward motion when applying products to the face and neck. Keep skin around the eyes moisturized to prevent dryness and wrinkles.

Shea butter, a fat derived from the seeds of the shea tree, has been noted as an excellent treatment for skin of color. Shea butter can help reduce cutaneous discoloration and promote healing. Shea butter is also used in certain foods, soaps and candles.

The Hands

Hands are the biggest indicator of age. Keep yours soft and attractive by applying lotion or cream constantly. Protect hands from excessive water, chemicals and detergents. *Always* wear latex gloves while cleaning and doing dishes. You can soothe tired hands with a weekly apricot kernel scrub. Lotion hands liberally afterwards and wear thin cotton gloves to bed.

The Feet

For some ungodly reason, men seem to have a real fixation with women's feet. This is quite curious since few men take care of their own feet. Nevertheless, it's to your advantage to keep feet pedicured and attractive. If you don't get pedicures regularly, lotion feet daily and remove dead skin weekly with a pumice stone or scraper. Also prevent athlete's foot by periodically using an antifungal spray whether you notice odor or not. Cut toenails square to avoid hang-nails.

Screen your Fragrances

Many women don't realize they may be wearing too many fragrances that can clash: perfume, deodorant, soap, hair pomade, lotion and powder. Before buying a new product, open it if possible and smell it. Mentally match it with the other products you're using: floral-scented lotion to use with floral cologne, for example. Unscented deodorant and lotions are ideal because they won't interfere with any other fragrance. Vanilla, cocoa butter and shea butter lotion are also good choices because they can compliment virtually *every* fragrance.

Tip: Some seductresses believe wearing a combination of light, fruity and herbal fragrances bolsters memory, energy and concentration.

Nails

Men are turned off by chipped nail polish on hands and feet. It's better to leave nails natural than to paint and neglect them. If you paint your nails, choose polish which reflects your mood: light frosts to appear cool and reticent, metallics for a futuristic or exotic effect, red to vamp him, black to dominate him. Don't let nails grow too long. If you interview several men, most will probably say they prefer women's nails neatly manicured at a moderate length.

Hair Removal Tips

Always shave in the same direction as hair growth to avoid razor bumps and ingrown hairs. After shaving the legs or armpits, apply witch hazel to close pores. If waxing, shower first to *open* pores, to make the process easier and less excruciating. If using cream depilatories, do so in moderation and alternate this method with shaving or waxing.

When tweezing brows, follow these rules to achieve maximum attractiveness:

Never tweeze above the brow line, always shape from underneath. Thick brows can be very sexy when shaped properly.

 Follow the natural shape of your brow. Use an eyebrow pencil to fill in gaps and further define the shape.

Tweezing a high arch opens the eyes and makes the face appear slimmer and/or more angular. A high arch can also give you a savvy and sophisticated look.

  Thin brows will generally make the eyes appear larger. This style however, may be outdated. Warning: If brows are tweezed too thin, your cute, well-proportioned forehead will become melon-like.

Make-Up

Make-up is a very special issue, since every woman's face is completely different. Some women have great bone structure for make-up, others need little or no cosmetics to look their best. Whether you're a simple eyeliner and lip gloss gal, or the type of seductress who goes the full yard with foundation, powder, etc., certain rules of seduction will still apply.

First things first. When planning a seduction ritual, decide what effect you plan to have on the man that day (or night). Will you be innocent, or will you be a vamp? Do you want to be cute, or do you plan to be kinky? Will you be exotic, or just plain erotic? Are you soft, or are you really sinful? Here are the general rules:

Quote of the Day: "Beauty is in the eye of the beer holder."

♥ Stick with soft colors (natural, skin tone, pastels) if you want to appear soft and somewhat innocent.

♥ Natural colors (flesh-tones) are unassuming and give a man the impression you're good natured, sincere and down to earth.

♥ Choose bold colors (reds, purples, black) if you want him to think you're bad to the bone.

Any effect you choose can turn a man on immensely. However, when you first seduce a male, it's better to start with the soft approach and work your way up to naughty. Here are a few other tips:

♥ Make-up for a night out on the town may be too heavy for an at-home seduction ritual.

♥ If you plan to sleep in your make-up, apply it lightly. Use cosmetics which don't smudge.

♥ While glossy lipstick makes lips appear succulent, it smears easily and stains quickly. Matte lipstick lasts longer. Good quality mattes won't smear, regardless of *what* you do with your lips.

♥ Brighten your eyes and make them sparkle by lining the bottom lids from corner to corner with a frosty blue or lavender pencil. To create a smoldering effect, draw a fine line on the lower lids with black Kohl pencil or liquid liner. Smudge and blend the line gently with a cotton swab. When lining the bottom lids, apply more color in the center and thin the line at the corners of your eyes.

♥ If you're into natural products, you might appreciate make-up which contains Green Tea powder. Green tea is derived from the Camellia sinensis plant and has been discovered to contain cancer-fighting, anti-oxidants. For this reason, green tea has become very popular as a dietary supplement and an additive for cosmetics.

Lip Synch

Black women have the sexiest mouths: full, luscious and ripe, no collagen or implants necessary. To increase the sex appeal of your most seductive orifice, draw a line just beyond your natural lip line using a pencil the same color as your lips. Fill in with your favorite lipstick or gloss. If you want to brighten your smile, try red, orange and brown lipstick colors.

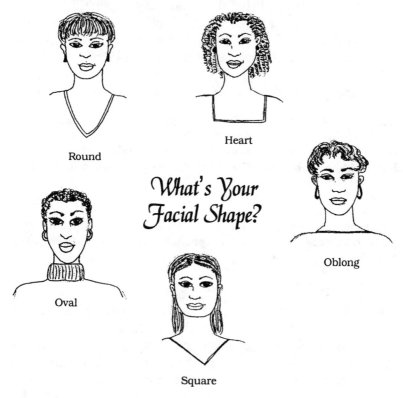

Round

Heart

What's Your Facial Shape?

Oval

Square

Oblong

Women of color are blessed with diverse beauty. No matter how your face is shaped, you can enhance your looks with carefully chosen necklines and jewelry.

Quote of the day: "Nobody's ugly after 2 a.m.!"

Adorn Yourself

Body adornment is both exotic and sexy. In addition to contemporary jewelry, try toe rings, belly chains or jewels in the navel, ankle bracelets and jewels in the hair. You can pretend to be an oriental princess, or the main attraction in a sultan's harem. Your only limit is your imagination. Whatever you choose will be ultra-stimulating for the man of your choice.

Body paint and glitter are also sexy. These items can be scented and/or flavored. Glitter can make you look and feel ethereal, like a goddess. Body adornments, paint and glitter go extremely well with sheer clothing.

Choose contemporary jewelry that will balance your features, considering facial shape, neck, and hairstyle.

For a round or full face: try ovals, drops, rectangle earrings. Avoid large, beaded necklaces and chokers.

Long, oblong/narrow face: wear square or round earrings.

Heart-shaped face: dangling earrings, drops, studs will suit you. Avoid large, round jewelry.

Square face: round shapes can soften the jaw line. Try circular and oval earrings, hoops and buttons.

Short/heavy neck: low neckline with long necklaces slim you down.

Long/thin neck: chokers and short chains add weight and volume.

Clothes Conscious

A seductress wears garments that will enhance her beauty. This doesn't mean the clothes are revealing, although revealing clothes can sometimes be the order of the day. A seductress knows men are often intrigued by what they *can't* see. So, she uses her knowledge of optical illusions to make her appear however she desires. Tips: Natural fabrics (cotton, silk, wool) are believed to enhance energy flow and stimulate the aura. When choosing colors for your garments, match them to your skin tone first, hair second. If you're changing your wardrobe, you might want to shop for make-up at the same time to ensure they compliment each other.

What colors to choose?

Cool colors: blues and greens (sky and leaf colors). Blue is the color of power and authority and flattering to most skin tones. Wear it when you want to take control. Green suggests relaxation and is also supposed to help concentration. Cool colors in dark tones can be weight absorbing and make you look slimmer.

Warm colors: earth tones (reds, yellows, oranges, browns, pinks and golds). Warm colors in dark tones, especially brown, optically reduce your size. Red, pink and orange create excitement and suggest an outgoing personality. Red also exudes confidence.

Neutral colors: black, white, beige and gray. Neutral colors match any skin tone and can balance an outfit either by creating a contrast or a blend. Black is elegant and mysterious, white is often perceived as innocent but can be revealing. Beige is easygoing, feminine and non-threatening, gray is calm, classy and collected.

Enhance what you have, conceal what you don't.

To appear taller and slimmer: Choose garments in cool or neutral colors and/or with vertical lines to keep the eye moving upward: coat/trench dresses, high neck tops and tops which cover the hips, pants with a flat front, single-breasted jackets and jackets which cover the hips. Vertical zippers, buttons from neck to hem and V necklines are also weight concealers. Wear a moderate heel to balance your figure and control lingerie and hosiery or body dress with full slip. Wear sleeves as long as they don't hug the upper arm.

Heavy women should avoid: clothes with a tight fit across the waistline or bust, belts and anything which makes the eye travel horizontally. Never let a skirt dip in under the stomach. Shiny fabrics which reflect light, such as satin and lycra will make you appear heavier, as will ruffles, beaded garments, embroidery and large, attention-grabbing patterns.

If you are very petit, avoid: stiletto heels, pants with cuffs, draw-string waistbands and skirts that are too short. Petit women look fantastic in: sleeveless, strapless and halter dresses, fitted tops and turtlenecks, slip dresses.

To conceal large or square shoulders: never wear shoulder pads. Draw attention from shoulders with a large lapel or collar.

To conceal large hips: Never wear tight, narrow skirts. Try wearing A-line or gored skirts. Draw the attention to your shoulders and neckline with lighter colors for your top, interesting collars V-necks and jewelry.

To reduce the size of your bust: minimizer bra, crossed wraparound bodice or any garment that forms a diagonal line across the bust. Darts at the shoulder can also release fullness across the bust.

To make your breasts appear larger and your figure more curvaceous: padded bras, curved lines over the bust, dresses with a yoke that has a shirring right at the bustline, shoulder pads, double-breasted jackets and dresses, breast pockets, thick textures, open neck tops and lighter colors, especially on top. Also: hip hugger pants, pleated pants, halter and slip dresses, A-line skirts.

To make yourself appear heavier and/or shorter: stress horizontal lines with belts. Wear gathered skirts and pleats, bulky pockets, two-color dresses, square necklines and boatnecks. Also choose shiny and satiny materials, velvet, pile and any other bulky textured fabric, plaids, large stripes, flowers or prints.

The Lair of the Seductress

When a man enters your lair, he is in *your* world. The lair of the seductress is always clean, cozy and inviting. If you choose your components carefully, you can enjoy versatility and change your den regularly. Each time the man enters, there'll be a new (and exciting) surprise in store. Each intriguing experience will make him want to return. Again and again.

You'll spend roughly a third of your life in bed, so create a bedroom that's wonderful. Give the room a feeling of sumptuousness and sensuality. Create it for *yourself* first, then add the finishing touches to seduce the male. You don't have to spend a lot of money. The key to a fabulous lair is to decorate tastefully and remember more is not always better.

The color of the walls will set the overall tone for the room. Avoid loud, gaudy colors because they are painful to the eyes and difficult to match. You achieve more flexibility with basic wall colors that you can dress up with accessories. Washable flat or satin paint are best for a bedroom. Semi-gloss tends to look pasty and gives the lair a less-than-opulent feel.

Choose linen, curtains and accessories just as you would your clothing: colors which flatter your skin, textures which feel good against your body. Remember these basic rules: dark colors are warm, mysterious and absorbing, and make a room look smaller. Light colors are cool, serene and reflective, and make a room appear larger. Florals and patterns suggest activity and while soothing, tend to be busy. Animal prints are wild and wicked, but don't overdo it.

Good linen is pricey, but worth it. If possible, opt for 200 plus thread count. Egyptian cotton is soft, but requires ironing. Permanent press is easier to care for, but not as luxurious. Some women scent their sheets and pillows lightly with perfume. This can inspire passion when done in moderation.

Lighting can make both you and the room appear more or less attractive. Bright overhead and fluorescent lights, reveal *everything*. Use lamps whenever possible and candles for ambiance. Arrange lamps so lighting is even throughout the room. Frosted pink bulbs are soft.

If you have a green thumb, invest in a few plants. Plants breathe life into a home and lift the spirits, are very romantic and relaxing. Try easy-care plants like Cactus, Lipstick, Peace Lily and Pothos.

There are many ways to accessorize your lair. Velvet, satin and lace throw pillows are a excellent choice as are items in wicker, ceramic, crystal, clay and wood. The entire room should speak your name and say something personal about you.

Being a seductress is work, but the payoff is large: you look great, feel great and have a wonderful sex life. For continued success, remember and adhere to these tried-and-true rules of seduction:

Rules of Seduction

♥ Decide what you want from a man before you pursue him. The reason: the way you get him is the way you'll have to keep him. Employ sex appeal for sex, personality for sincerity, friendship for spirituality.

♥ When you meet a new man, don't reveal too much about yourself too quickly. A little mystery is always intriguing. Relax and let the relationship progress at a comfortable pace.

♥ Let the man talk to his heart's content about his life, his accomplishments, etc. When a man first meets a woman, he tries to present the best portrait of himself. If you view his portrait favorably, he'll feel closer to you.

♥ Men love women who *apparently* love them. Make him believe he's the greatest and you admire him more than any other man you've ever met.

♥ If you love him, never reveal too much of your emotions. Keep him guessing. If he becomes too comfortable, he may neglect you or take advantage.

♥ If you pursue him, pursue him passively. There's an expression: "He chased me until I caught him." Let him feel he is the aggressor and make him want you.

♥ Men despise what they obtain too easily. If he feels there's no challenge in you, he'll be inclined to lose interest. Don't be too available and make him aware you're both in demand and up for grabs.

♥ Let him compete for your interest. If you have a busy life, are always on the go and doing something positive, he'll work harder to get your attention.

♥ Always keep him wanting more by *never* giving him all he wants. Fill his bowl halfway and he'll stay hungry.

ℛelated ℛesources

Coping with Difficult People by Robert M. Bramson, PH.D., Anchor Books, Doubleday. ISBN: 0-385-17362-8.

The Principles of Seduction by G. Clayton Viddler, Pedestal Press. ISBN: 0-9627602-6-9.

Another Page in my Personal Chapter...

Beauty comes from within. Suggestions: If I could change something about my appearance, what would it be and why? How can I learn to like myself better the way I am? What would make me look and feel more beautiful?

_____

_____

_____

_____

_____

_____

_____

_____

_____

_____

_____

_____

_____

_____

_____

This is YOUR personal page. Write on! ✎ *More space on the reverse...*

Oils, Wax and Scents for Love
Tools of the Mystical Seductress

A Mystical Seductress is a special woman, intrinsically connected to nature and the earth. Deeply spiritual, she is perceptive to everything around her. She uses natural resources to appeal to the senses, inspire love and evoke feelings of joy. For many men, she is sensual, mysterious and irresistible.

This chapter offers you illuminating secrets of enticement, ancient tools to enrapture the male of your choice. *Oils, wax and Scents for Love* is not a study of the occult nor does it involve the worship of any deities. A more detailed exploration of mystical seduction can be found in my second work, *The Mystical Seductress Handbook*, available from Swing Street Publishing.

Mystical Oils

Mystical oils work when you believe in them. If you feel sexy, you will be sexy. If you feel desirable, men will desire you. Mystical oils are most commonly found in religious stores and should not be confused with Essential Oils*. In this section, I have listed the most powerful mystical oils used in the game of love and their specific purposes. Before we begin however, let's review some common-sense precautions:

Consult your doctor or health care professional before trying any new products on your body. If you ever experience an allergic reaction to an oil, discontinue use and consult a physician. Never ingest oils unless they have been labeled safe for consumption or you've received approval from your doctor, professional aromatherapist or herbalist. Do not place oils inside of mucous membranes or orifices unless instructed by a licensed health care professional. Do not use oils on small children or animals.

Which Oil to Choose?

Any oil you select should work well for you. However, some oils are of particular benefit to certain astrological signs. As a general rule, if the name or fragrance of an oil attracts you, it is probably made for you. Don't be afraid to experiment. You have *Delilah Power!*

ADAM AND EVE: One on one excitement. If you place some of this oil on your beloved, he or she will be yours forever. Win over a shy man by anointing your neck and wrists. Great for Air signs and women who enjoy playing the temptress.

APHRODESIA: The oil of yearning passion and sex. To feel and appear sexier, place a small drop between the breasts and across the thighs. Earth-shattering orgasms await you. Water signs receive extra assistance.

ARABIAN NIGHTS: If placed on the man's body before bed, Arabian Nights will ignite spellbinding ecstasy and prolong the sexual encounter. Take care not to use too much of this oil at one time. It's effect is supposedly stronger than Viagra.

ATTRACTION: Resolve conflict in a current relationship, bring an old love back to you or captivate someone new. Attraction oil assures success. Dress a red candle to lure a man from someone else, if you dare. Air signs benefit greatly.

BERRY OF FISH: Many people report great success using this oil just before "Doing the Nasty". Berry of Fish makes the man last a long time. Just what a growing girl needs!

CEDAR: Use this oil to help build your confidence when you want to approach a man who is reserved in nature. Good for Earth signs.

CINNAMON: An oil that attracts horny men. Place three drops in the bath to get your boots knocked. For more power, soak cinnamon bark in the oil prior to use. Earth signs see increased benefits.

CLEOPATRA: The royal oil of seduction. Use Cleopatra to powerfully attract the lover you desire and make him your slave. Use it to anoint bed accessories for enhanced sexual pleasure and repeat performances. Fire signs benefit greatly.

CLOVER: If you want fidelity, place a few drops on the pillow of the one you adore and he will remain faithful and true. For increased potency, soak a few clover plants in the oil.

CLOVES: Place on the throat and thighs. Put a small drop between the knees. This oil will excite your mate, or the lover you desire. This is a very strong love oil. Use with caution!

COCONUT: Coconut oil inspires positive feelings. Use a few drops in the bath, on your favorite candle, or with incense. Anoint the hair, ankles and hips. Make him pleasure you with his lips.

FIRE: Ignites lust. To revive a dead sex life, place a small drop on your man's washcloth before he takes his shower.

FLAME OF DESIRE: Like the phoenix who burns itself only to rise again, your lover can be trapped in your blistering spell until you choose to release him. For Fire signs.

GINGER OIL: Men love optimism. Ginger helps to keep you optimistic, thus making each day more enjoyable.

HONEYSUCKLE: Attracts money, business and the opposite sex. Place on the wrists and behind the ears.

HUMMINGBIRD: Delicate as the bird it is named after, this oil reveals your sweet vulnerability. A small drop to the hairs of the pubic triangle arouses the one who loves you.

ISIS: Evokes the power of the Egyptian goddess Isis. Anoint the forehead and a white candle for assistance in all matters.

JASMINE: The goddess of love will come to your aid if you anoint your candle and bath water with this oil.

JEZEBEL: For the woman who wants to have her way with men. Use, abuse and spank him when he's naughty. Anoint the breasts, scalp and inner thighs to become the ultimate dominatrix and make him obey.

KHUS KHUS: If your lover has left you, using this oil could help win him back. Dress a red candle and burn for seven days. Anoint the chest area, covering the heart daily.

LA FLAMME: What should you do when the man you desire puts up tremendous resistance? Anoint your abdomen before going to bed. His resistance should weaken immediately. Also use La Flamme on a man who's giving you grief. Freeze the oil an hour before use to cool him out completely.

LAVENDER: Clears the mind and promotes mature love. Anoint a blue candle to attract an established, older man.

LILAC: Reach a man through his intuitive mind. Anoint a white candle. Also an effective meditation aid.

LIME: This is the oil of fidelity and devotion. Sprinkle a few drops of Lime oil on a frequently-used item. The owner of the item will be totally faithful and attentive to you.

LOTUS: This oil's scent is inspired by a beautiful, Egyptian flower. It is used to secure the affections of a fickle lover.

LYANG LYANG: If you want to be the ultimate tease, this is your oil. You should however, be ready to deliver!

MINT: Mint oil promotes positive change and advancement. Add to the bath or a floor wash. Extra benefits for Fire signs.

MOSS: If you want to manage your finances better, this oil can help. It can secure your financial position and prevent you from spending frivolously or unwittingly losing money.

MUSK: Dusky and sensual, Musk oil is a favorite of many. It can give you the strength, confidence and endurance needed to tackle your obstacles. It also inspires love and affection.

MYRTLE: If you ever find yourself in love with someone who wants only to be friends, this oil can be of benefit. Dress a pink candle and burn for several days. Good for Earth signs.

MYSTIC: Mystic creates the illusion of a changed appearance. Become a one-woman harem. Men you target will gravitate to you, believing there's something new and exciting about you each time they see you. Little do they know it's the power of Mystic and your mind drawing them in. It will be impossible for them to resist you.

NARCISSUS: Narcissus makes you feel more beautiful and alluring. If you place a drop on your pillow, you will awaken with new confidence. Also place a drop on your mirror.

NATURE: There are times when you may not want love from a man. In fact, you may only want sex. But, you want the sex to be sizzling hot, long-lasting and satisfying. Nature oil has intense sexual powers and can position you for a night of lustful coupling. Use it with a black candle and watch those big, strapping men draw to you like flies to molasses. At that point, you can have whatever you want from whomever you want. At your pace, on your terms.

NINE MYSTERIES: Learn secrets. Uncover deceit and expose the insincere. Place a drop in the center of the forehead.

NUTMEG: Nutmeg is used to deflect negativity from outside sources, such as when dealing with jealous friends.

OBEAH: Find out what your man is doing behind your back. Apply oil to your temples and dress a yellow candle.

ORANGE: One of the most powerful tools of attraction, Orange oil is a preferred choice of women on the prowl. Use it in the bath and on places where your pulse beats. Sprinkle a few drops in your candle. You will become a stud magnet.

ORANGE BLOSSOM: For those wishing to marry. Powerful when used in combination with Orange oil and a red candle. If the man is very resistant, try adding Cleopatra oil, Clover and Cloves. Great benefits for Water signs.

ORCHID: If men feel you are too aggressive, the exotic scent of this oil can help you to soften your approach.

ORRIS: Beginners in the love arena should try this oil when wishing to gain control. Also used to seduce a younger man.

QUEEN OF SHEBA: Solicit the powers of this great queen. She was beautiful, worldly and wise. You can use this oil to influence friends, entice lovers and solidify the affections of your husband. Air signs receive extra benefit.

ROSE OIL: If you wish to be subtle with a man, choose Rose Oil. This oil gently works its powers on the one you desire, winning him over without his knowledge.

SESAME: Sesame oil can be used to steal someone else's lover. Be cautious when undertaking such a venture. The laws of Cause and Effect maintain someone else may do the same to you one day!

TIGER OIL: If your man no longer has the "eye of the tiger" and has instead become a pussycat (in the negative sense of the word), then you desperately need this oil. Stimulate his animal nature and make him growl for you. Apply a touch of this oil to your breasts and hips. Massage some into his shoulders and arms. Watch him come alive, hungry for meat!

VANILLA: Be soft, sweet, gentle and sexy. Vanilla blends well with many other oils and is more potent with cinnamon. It also brings tranquility into the home environment.

VENUS: This is the oil of new and renewed relationships. Old friends draw closer and new friends miraculously appear. As Venus is the goddess of love, so will your man feel more devoted to you. All astrological signs will reap the benefits.

WHITE LAVENDER: White Lavender helps promote love and friendship. Anoint the hands, arms and feet after a sensual bath. If on the other hand, your passions burn too intensely and you need control, use White Lavender to cool sexual urges and temper your activities. Good for Water signs.

WHITE ROSE: A happy marriage can be yours with the proper use of this oil. White Rose oil is known to encourage inner peace and understanding, discourage conflict and discord and strengthen the bonds of love. All signs benefit.

WILD DESIRE: Whatever you desire can be yours, if you only believe. Wear this oil behind the ears and on the hair. Anoint a candle or place in the bath. Scent your bed linen for a hot romp. Fire signs are electrified.

Author's Note:

 There are many exciting uses for Mystical Oils, as you have seen in this section. Please keep in mind the modern practice of using mystical oils is loosely based on ancient beliefs and has no scientific foundation whatsoever. This information is provided solely for your entertainment.

* If you'd like to learn more about essential oils/aromatherapy, read: *The Mystical Seductress Handbook* by Tannis Blackman, Swing Street Publishing. ISBN: 0-9652540-5-4.

Aromatherapy for Healing the Spirit by Gabriel Mojay, An Owl Book. ISBN: 0-8050-4496-5.

Exotica

Meltdown:
Pleasure in the Mystique of Wax.

Why are candles so fascinating? What is it about them that holds us spellbound? Is it true candles can make a man incredibly horny?

Candles are, and have always been, a tremendous mood enhancer for people, particularly men.

When a man comes into your home, ready to make love and you light a candle for him, you are telling him that you plan to ignite his wick and you expect your wax to be melted in return. Men love candles because they lend an aura of mystery to the encounter. As the wax becomes softer, the man becomes harder. He just can't help himself.

One of the great things about candlelight is it can conceal all those lumps and bumps you try to hide from your man. You know, those cellulite-ridden areas most of us have somewhere. Most of you women out there know what areas I'm talking about. If you have any qualms about making love with the lights on, then candles are definitely for you. Men love to watch women during sex. Unfortunately, we don't always want to be watched, especially when our bodies don't look the way we want them to. With candles, your body appears super smooth, super soft and super sexy. You can be clearly seen at all angles, but you don't feel scrutinized. You can relax, show off your incredibly sexy body and rock his world. As they say, it's all in the presentation!

You'll be amazed by what a little creativity and a candle can do. Your essence and positive vibrations will make the candle work an unforgettable magic. Before we delve into the many ways you can use a candle to your advantage, please note these basic candle safety rules:

Always inspect your candles for cracks or chips prior to purchase and use. Choose a candle with a perfectly centered wick and keep the wick centered as the candle burns. Place lighted candles on a heat resistant surface and never leave candles burning unattended. Never burn candles near curtains, rugs, or other fabrics nor put lighted candles on the floors or in walkways. Keep your burning candles out of drafts. Never burn candles within reach of small children and discontinue use when an inch of candle wax remains.

Getting the Most out of Your Candle

Dress your candle whenever possible. If you are using a candle that is not already scented, or if you would like to enhance the power and fragrance of a candle, you can personalize it with your favorite oil(s). You 'dress' your candle by placing the oil on the wax prior to burning. See *Mystical Oils* for information on specific oils and their effects. When you dress a candle, you plant your essence and vibrations in it. The candle becomes your personal tool and will respond to your suggestions with greater urgency.

Helpful hints: Put your candles in the freezer for 1-2 hours before lighting to prolong burning time. When anointing a candle, use only a few drops of oil. Too much oil can saturate the wick and prevent the candle from burning properly.

Some believe that gray or black sediment on a candle indicates interference or obstacles in your path.[1] If you observe excessive sediment on a candle, it may be best to discard it. If a candle extinguishes itself prematurely, do not relight it. Wait 24 hours and light a new candle.

Candle Colors

Following is a listing of different candle colors you can buy, their mystical benefits and properties. Any candle

[1] Although unsightly, Black sediment on a candle is not necessarily dangerous and probably caused by a defective wick.

can suit your needs, but certain colors are considered more effective when burned for specific purposes. If you are attracted to a particular candle color, it is probably meant for you. When selecting a candle, look for and avoid many air bubbles in the wax.

Black: Scorpio men love this candle. An excellent candle to use for problem solving. Black creates an aura of intensity. It is a very erotic color. Use it to seduce a man, to draw ideas, or for profound contemplation. When a woman burns a Black candle for a Black man, he will do some very kinky things. Try lighting this candle on a Friday or Saturday night to get that party started.

Brown: An earthy, natural candle, great for attracting people born under the astrological sign of Aries as well as Earth signs Taurus and Virgo. Burn this candle for improvements at the job. Ignite a brown candle on a Thursday evening and your man will yearn to take you much like the stallion takes his mare.

Dark Blue: For serenity. Dark blue candles are enchanting and regal. Reminiscent of the ocean and its endless depths, this sensual color invites calm and soothes. Dark blue candles also promote personal wealth. This candle works well on Capricorn males. Burn a dark blue candle when you want him to worship you like a queen and behave like a man of royalty. He will exhibit class, good taste and a penchant for oral sex. What more can a woman ask?

Gold/Yellow: Enlivens your mood and brighten your surroundings. A friendly color. A gold candle can also be burned when you want to nurture your finances, improve your platonic relationships or create a friendly atmosphere with a man you've recently met. You can also cool down a man who is too eager.

Green: Often associated with money, green is a serene color. It is also the color of nature and new beginnings. Spring is a very green period of the year. A green candle urges expansion and fertility. It is also good for professional growth. Burn a green candle when you desire a man who has money. He will be happy to spend on you.

Gray: Used to eliminate negative influences and thoughts and smooth out difficulties you may be experiencing in your life at the moment. Gray candles are not as pretty as some of the other colors, but they are nice candles to burn on any occasion. They are stable influencers and can often promote responsibility and reliability. If you have a man on your hands that is high-strung, this candle will help stabilize him. Burn at dusk and dawn.

Lavender: Lavender candles create light, pleasant thoughts. An excellent candle to burn for relaxation. Light a lavender candle on Sunday if you wish to connect spiritually and emotionally with someone. This beautiful candle can be a handy tool for attracting the Air Signs, particularly Libra.

Light Blue: Light blue is soft. Gentle. A light blue candle is great to burn on a rainy day for it lifts the mood. This is a candle to burn when attracting the water signs, particularly Cancer. You can also burn this candle when you are feeling coy and want to tease your lover. Try lighting a pastel blue candle during a weekend, in the morning.

Multi-colored: A combination of candle color qualities, this candle is exotic and works extremely well with Pisces. Ignite this candle when you are feeling especially naughty or want some variety in your life. Anoint with an oil and multiply your intended effect. Multi-colored candles are great, all-around candles you can use in any situation.

Orange: The color of desire. Orange draws the attention of men, horny men in particular. Orange is bright, hot and cheerful. Orange candles are often used to draw people whose sun signs are Fire signs (Aries, Leo and Sagittarius). It is a very alluring color. Burn this candle when you feel cute and flirtatious, preferably on a Tuesday or Thursday afternoon.

Pink: Are you feeling coquettish? Pink is a feminine color that can generate affection and romance. It is a good candle for tapping into the gentler side of you. It is a youthful, energetic color. Pink is a nice colored candle to burn just after moving into a new apartment. Feign innocence or bring out the little girl in you with a man who wants to be your "Big Daddy". When anointed with the proper oils, pink candles are said to attract people born under the sign of Aquarius. You can also use this color to seduce a boy just past the age of jail bait, that is, if you have the nerve!

Peach: Peach is pleasing. It is a candle color that can coincide well with new beginnings. Peach candles are fresh and optimistic, great to burn if you are thinking of starting a new relationship or job. If you light a peach candle when the right man is present, you will make him want to devour you like dessert. The best day to burn this candle: Saturday.

Purple: A sumptuous color which encourages passion and profound thoughts, for meditative people wishing to explore psychic abilities. Purple candles are also stunning. Burn this color candle if you are in the mood to mesmerize your lover. This candle creates a unique atmosphere that makes you ravishing. Your lovemaking will be intense, spiritual and long lasting. Best days to light this candle: Monday and Wednesday.

Red: The color of love, sex and vibrant health. Red is intense and passionate. It represents the heart and blood which pulse within you. It is a sexy color that creates lust and desire. This is a terrific candle to burn when you are planning the type of romantic evening that leaves both you and your lover gasping for breath. For a double whammy, wear red undergarments, red lipstick and a red ribbon in your hair. Serve red wine.

White: Used to promote clarity of thought. The absence of color in this candle eliminates the power of outside influences. This is a good color to choose if you are confused about an issue. White candles are also seductive in a subtle way. They are said to attract people born under the Air signs and create a spiritual aura that helps you to connect to the other person. Light this color candle to make a man think of marriage. If you light a white candle before sex, your lovemaking will be tender and emotional.

Now that you know The Secrets…

Take full advantage of what candles have to offer. Tap into the secret powers of wax to fulfill your ultimate desires and have fun! You can do some enticing things with a candle and a bit of imagination. Let your imagination run wild!

Once you've gotten into the habit of using candles, you'll find them to be an integral part of your normal routine. Light a candle every time you take a bath or if you want an emotional lift. Light a candle for someone who is ill, or a friend who needs support. Light a candle for the man you love to let him know he is the light of your life. Whatever the reason, your positive energies and the candles you burn will brighten any day!

Heaven Scent
Aroma Remedies for The Soul

 In previous pages, you discovered how mystical oils and candles can positively influence your love life. In this section, you'll be introduced to natural fragrances that can fill your mind with wonder, lift the spirits and reveal your Higher Self. Aroma Remedies can help you appeal to men on a profound, subconscious level, encouraging spiritual love and burning passion. Nature has provided us with tools we can use to improve our physical and mental conditions. Let's take advantage of them. After all, they're heaven scent!

NATURAL SOURCE	KEY WORD
Vanilla bean/extract	*Serenity*
Cinnamon bark	*Excitement*
Whole cloves	*Attraction*
Eucalyptus branch	*Clarity*
Rose/rose concentrate	*Affection*
Lavender oil	*Calm*
Orange (fruit)	*Passion*
Nutmeg	*Positivity*
Lemon (rind)	*Uplifting*
Lime (rind)	*Energy*

The natural sources you see above will be used in three aroma remedies that are simple to prepare, yet immensely powerful. If you meditate regularly and/or engage in prayer, you can increase the power of both by adding an aroma remedy. Now, reread the list and as you do so, say the key word for each natural source aloud. Afterwards, recite the following affirmation:

"I am perfect, whole and complete. My world is in sublime order and my life is divinely guided. I release all negativity and allow my positive energies to flow within me. All that I need, want and hope for, is and always will be, provided."

Exotica

Aroma Remedy #1: Mental Stimulator
Prepare this remedy shortly before bed or meditation/prayer

Rind of 1 lemon, cut into small pieces
Rind of 1 lime, cut into strips
Eucalyptus branch, crumbled
Metal Steamer

Mix items together, place in steamer and steam uncovered for 1-2 minutes. Remove immediately from heat and transfer to a glass bowl. Set bowl near bedside. Lasts several days.

Aroma Remedy #2: Soul Rejuvenator

10 drops rosewater concentrate
1 teaspoon Vanilla Extract
1 cup water
A small piece of vanilla bean (less than an inch)
Petals of one rose
Pinch of fresh lavender or lavender oil
Pinch of fresh nutmeg, ground

In a small pot, bring water, rosewater concentrate, vanilla extract, vanilla bean and nutmeg to a boil. Immediately remove from heat. Breathe vapors for a few moments as solutions cools. When solution has reached a lukewarm temperature, add rose petals and lavender oil. Transfer to a glass dish and place at bedside.

Seducing with Scents

When a man enters your home and he is greeted by pleasant fragrances, the cool, smell of eucalyptus, or the warm spice of cinnamon apple for example, he finds himself wanting to linger. He finds himself reminded of happy times and wonderful feelings. He suddenly finds himself very attracted to you. Without knowing why, he suddenly wants to remove his shoes and socks, loosen his belt and tune into nature.

Tuning into nature can mean having hot animalistic sex! Why? Because one of man's primal, instincts is to procreate and reproduce. You might not be ready to reproduce, but you want that man to hit it like there's no tomorrow! Your mission: keep his nose open!

> *Man + Sensual Odors + You = Serious Turn On!*
> *Serious Turn On = Hot, Animalistic Sex!*
> *Hot, Animalistic Sex = Amazing Orgasms for You!*

This is a very simple equation to remember. Not as brilliant as the Theory of Relativity, nor the kind of math you learned in school, but a fool proof way to get what you desire. And what fun!

Decide which way you want to go. Do you want to be mysterious, or mischievous? Do you want to clear the man's mind, or fill his head with raw, sexual thoughts? Relax or energize him, make him giddy with desire, or insane with lust? The choice is yours!

Aroma Remedy #3: Love Generator

1 large orange, unpeeled
15-20 fresh cloves
Small hook
A yard of ribbon

Stick the cloves into the rind of the orange, spacing them evenly apart. Insert the hook into the base of the orange and use the ribbon to hang near your bedside. A delightful, natural air freshener that will attract love and last for weeks.

  ## Feeling Incensed

Incense was invented in Africa by ancient Egyptians who burned them during religious ceremonies. It is said that Cleopatra VII used incense, among other things, to charm, mesmerize and excite her lovers. You, too, have the power to excite, mesmerize and charm. Because you have *Delilah Power!* you can now use incense to your own sensual advantage.

When incense and candles are combined, your powers of seduction are augmented. If you burn incense with a particular man in mind, you place your suggestions into the air. If receptive, he will receive your suggestions in his subconscious and he will invariably respond. Your desires will envelope him like a gentle cloud and make him think of you, no matter where he is.

When the man comes to visit you and you light incense, he will sit there, wondering what you have in store for him. His eyes will follow you as you move around your domain, much like a cheetah stalking an unsuspecting gazelle. His breaths will quicken, his mouth will become dry and his hands will yearn to touch you. He will be at the brink of surrender. Shortly thereafter, the man will close his eyes, inhale the sweet aroma and realize he's got to have you.

If you are working with incense and candles together, there is a way to maximize the powers of both: in secrecy, light your incense first, then use the flame from the incense to ignite your candle. Let the smoke from the incense surround the wick as it burns down to the wax. Next, swirl the incense around the candle, taking care not to touch the wax. Fill your mind with whatever it is you desire. Finally, scent your glowing aura with the incense by swirling the smoking stick around your body, holding its lighted end at arm's distance, avoiding clothes and hair.

As you experiment with incense, you'll find many of the fragrances correspond with scented oils. To preserve the freshness and integrity your incense, store them in an air tight container. The three fragrances below are manufactured in India and have been known to produce very positive results: **Nag Champa** and **Super Hit** by Satya Sai Baba, **Precious Chandan** by Hem.

Playing with Potpourri

Scented potpourri has become very popular due to its decorative appearance and assortment of fragrances. Placed in a glass bowl and left to air, potpourri can add a natural tranquility to the home environment. To use potpourri for seduction, position it near your bed, or on your night table.

- For an inexpensive, easy to make sachet, stuff your favorite potpourri in an old stocking or pantyhose and place in a drawer.
- Fill an old shoe box with potpourri, poke holes and place in the closet.
- Fill an empty vase with potpourri instead of flowers.
- Make your own simmering potpourri: boil a cup or two of water in an old, unused pot. Add potpourri and let simmer or transfer to a heavy-duty ceramic dish. Vapors will permeate the air gracefully.
- Purchase a lamp ring and fill with potpourri oil or your favorite mystical oil. Each time you turn on the light, the heat from the light bulb will warm the oil and release its odors into the air.

Note: When it comes to potpourri, you get what you pay for. Although pricey, quality potpourri is made from fruits, herbs and spices and will retain its fragrance. Potpourri costing a dollar in discount stores is usually made from scented wood shavings which collect dust and lose the scent quickly.

Author's Note:

The information is this section uniquely explores how natural stimuli can affect the emotions and should not be confused with aromatherapy. If you'd like to learn more about aromatherapy, consult a licensed aromatherapist.

Another Page in my Personal Chapter..

It's time to show that man what you're made of. A kinky suggestion: Devise a seduction ritual in which you are the master. What will you do to him from the moment he walks through the door, to the second he collapses in your arms?

_____

_____

_____

_____

_____

_____

_____

_____

_____

_____

_____

_____

_____

_____

_____

_____

_____

_____

Best of luck and many blessings. Write on! ✎ *More space on reverse...*

Crystal Clear
Channeling Crystal Energy

This chapter introduces you to the power of crystals and shows you ways to channel crystal energy. Many people have enlightened their minds, improved their overall health and discovered a special tranquility by wearing crystals. Channeling crystal energy is a very personal process which may not be for everyone. If you can appreciate having a positive influence in your life, wearing beautiful stones and exploring a timeless mystery, then the information in this chapter may be very helpful.

According to traditional yoga philosophy, the human body has several points of energy which activate and command it. These points are called *chakras* which, in Sanskrit means "wheels". The concept of channeling crystal energy is fairly simple. Picture the way an antenna helps a television or radio tune into a station. Because crystals produce electrical impulses, many people believe wearing them over the chakras can help to achieve energy balance. In effect, you use crystals to tune into and strengthen your own energy force.

There are many different types of crystals, each stone having its own special properties and recognized uses. When shopping for a crystal, you may find your eyes drawn to a particular stone. This is an unconscious process that can mean the crystal has a power you need. There are no set rules for choosing a crystal. Just free your mind, listen to your inner voice and buy the stone that attracts you. The best place to search for crystals is at a wholesale importer. There you will find larger selections and better quality stones.

After purchasing a crystal, there are a few steps you can take to fully utilize its powers. It is beneficial to clean your crystal, clear it and then program it. This makes the crystal personal and allows it to work its magic for you in an intimate and unencumbered way.

The Chakras

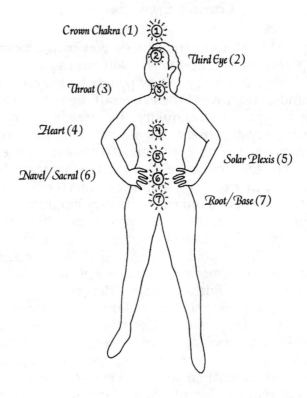

Crown Chakra (1)

Third Eye (2)

Throat (3)

Heart (4)

Solar Plexis (5)

Navel/Sacral (6)

Root/Base (7)

To clean your crystal, rinse it for a few moments in cool, clear water or water enriched with natural sea salt. You can also soak the crystal in salt water or dip it in the ocean. To clear a crystal, place it directly in the sun's light for about an hour. The sun's energy will remove all previous programming and clear the crystal's channels, preparing it for the suggestions you intend to make.

Programming a crystal is very easy. All you need is a bit of concentration and a few minutes of undisturbed time. The purpose of programming a crystal is to instill your thoughts, feelings and desires within the stone's molecular structure. As the crystal's molecules vibrate, your own positive energy is augmented, increasing your ability to accomplish your goals.

Hold the crystal in one hand and close your eyes. Focus on what you want the crystal to do for you. Ask it to give you the positive energy you need to overcome your obstacles. Think of sending positive vibrations into the stone. Visualize all you want to obtain and achieve. Continue meditating in this way for as long as you feel necessary. Some people can program a crystal in a few seconds, others need several minutes. When your feel the programming is complete, simply wear or pocket your crystal and enjoy the wonderful emanations.

Crystals and the Aura

Your aura is an energy field which surrounds your body like an egg-shaped cloud. Each person's aura is unique and has colors that can fluctuate according to the person's mood, health and mental condition. The average aura extends approximately three feet from the body and can be photographed using a special process known as Kirlian Photography. Some people claim they can see the aura with the naked eye and know how a person is feeling at any given moment. It is believed wearing crystals helps balance the aura and increase its brightness, thus improving mental and physical health.

Helpful Tips

Wear your crystal with a leather or satin cord rather than a metal chain, because metal can sometimes disrupt energy flow. Clean, clear and reprogram your crystal periodically. Do not allow many others to touch or play with your crystal. Once you've programmed your crystal, it is your personal tool and should not be exposed to potentially negative energy.

Types of Crystals and their Benefits

Amber: Amber is a fossilized resin which comes from prehistoric trees. This elegant, brown crystal is said to stimulate the intellect, balance the spiritual self and warm the emotions. It is also good for the muscles. Place over the solar plexus, navel, crown and third eye chakras. Also place under your pillow or mattress.

Amethyst: A beautiful, clear, lavender stone of the quartz variety, Amethyst is one of the most powerful crystals you can buy. It is used for meditation and to increase psychic ability. It is also used to aid in the healing of mental disorders. Anywhere you place this crystal will be beneficial. If you plan to cover the chakras, try the crown, third eye, throat and heart. Amethyst is also believed to strengthen the endocrine, circulatory and immune systems, cleanse the blood, stimulate the kidneys and strengthen the heart.

Aquamarine: Aquamarine is a purifying stone often worn to improve the circulatory system and glands. It releases fears and phobias and attracts love. Wear over the throat chakra.

Aventurine: Aventurine is an opaque, green stone which resembles jade. It promotes tranquility as well as positive mental and emotional processes. Most powerful when worn over the heart chakra.

Carnelian: A brownish red, opaque stone in the chalcedony family. Its properties are similar to those of the Bloodstone. Carnelian is most powerful when worn over the heart, solar plexus or navel. Carnelian enriches the blood, warms the emotions and aligns the physical and mental bodies.

Citrine: A clear, yellow stone, in the quartz family. Aligns you with your higher consciousness and increases your ability to heal yourself. Place over your crown chakra or navel.

Garnet: Garnet promotes love, passion and sex. It is most beneficial when placed or worn over the root chakra. It also has regenerative properties for the entire body.

Hematite: A smooth, black stone with a pearly surface. Hematitie is an excellent stone for a male. It is beneficial for the bloodstream and increases sexual potency.

Jade: Jade is worn for courage and wisdom, longevity and fertility. Believed to aid in feminine disorders. Wear over the navel.

Jasper: This stone can come in a variety of colors. It is easily recognizable by its beautiful and irregular colored markings. Jasper is in the chalcedony family and is considered helpful to internal organs such as the bladder, liver and kidneys. Carry Jasper in your pocket or wear around the stomach.

Lapis Lazuli: A rich, dark blue stone with small markings. Wearing Lapis Lazuli can increase your psychic and intuitive abilities and help you to bond with your spirit guides. Good for the skeletal system, the thyroid and adrenal glands.

Obsidian: Obsidian is actually a form of volcanic glass. Its surface is very smooth, shiny and black. Obsidian is thought to promote longevity and virility. Increases sex drive.

Onyx: This black stone is smooth, glossy and dense in color. This is a man's stone. Onyx improves strength, power and conviction, promotes maturity and increases passion.

Opal: This white, iridescent stone is mysterious and breathtaking. It has numerous positive qualities. However, some believe it is bad luck to buy an opal for oneself. Opal is a stone that should always be given and received as a gift.

Quartz (Clear): Crystal Quartz is the ideal stone to use to increase mental capacity and rejuvenate human tissue. Tourmalinated Quartz, Smoky Quartz and Rutilated Quartz are variations with similar properties.

Rose Quartz: Considered the love stone, Rose Quartz is pink and opaque. Rose Quartz is often worn when attempting to draw love and affection. Rose Quartz helps to release negative emotions such as jealousy, rage, guilt and resentment. Best worn over the heart chakra.

Tiger Eye: This stone is ideal for a man. It increases strength and vigor, fortifies personal convictions and enhances virility. Tiger Eye is also beneficial for the colon, digestive system, spleen and pancreas. For women: best worn over the heart and navel. For men: wear over the navel and/or solar plexus.

Topaz (Yellow and Blue): To increase creativity and release negativity. Helps you to communicate with your spirit guides and find answers to difficult questions. Helps clarify dreams.

Turquoise: Native Americans knew the value and beauty of this stone and used it to make weapons and jewelry. Turquoise aligns the chakras and allows for intense meditation. Wear this stone to achieve mental balance and emotional stability.

There are many other stones which can be of great benefit in channeling crystal energy, this is only a partial listing. For a more comprehensive explanation of crystals, their properties and ways to use crystals for healing, or if you'd like to explore channeling crystal energy further, check out the related resources below.

Related Resources

Aura Energy for Health, Healing and Balance by Joe H. Slate, PH.D.,Llewellyn Publications. ISBN: 1-56718-637-8.

Crystal Healing by Phyllis Galde, Llewellyn Publications, ISBN: 0-87542-246-2.

Healing and The Mind by Bill Moyers, published by Doubleday. ISBN: 0-385-46870-9.

The Chakras & Esoteric Healing by Zachary F. Lansdowne, Ph.D. Samuel Weiser, Inc. ISBN: 0-87728-584-5.

The Mystical Seductress Handbook by Tannis Blackman, Swing Street Publishing. ISBN: 0-9652540-5-4.

Today's Quote: "I don't suffer from insanity, I enjoy every minute of it."

Mind over Matter
Using Creative Vision to Achieve your Goals

 This section will show you ways to use positive thinking to achieve your goals. At the same time, you'll learn to strengthen your mind, tap your creative energies and conquer many of your fears.

Creative Vision is a technique involving several steps, beginning with the use of your mind's eye to visualize what you want as though it *already exists*. Creative Vision is more than fantasizing or daydreaming, and nothing like an hallucination, which is a distorted view of reality. Creative Vision is governed by right thinking and right actions. It works by creating a cycle of energy around you that can act as a magnet to attract whatever it is you want.

Most people think seeing is believing, but what one sees can often be deceiving. Thus, many beliefs are based on illusions. The reality is, *believing is seeing.* By envisioning something in your mind, you obtain the ability to manifest it in your life.

Creative Vision Part 1: Solid Confirmations. Rather than ask the universe for what you want, openly confirm your desires like you've *already obtained them.* What you confirm can and will become a part of your experience. Say the same confirmations daily. You'll be amazed by how quickly your life can change and the obstacles which seemed insurmountable to you before begin to dissolve.

When composing a confirmation, think positively. Do not focus on harming others, or engaging in acts which are morally wrong or questionable. You shouldn't ask the universe for someone else's husband or seek revenge on a person. This is about positive growth and change. Remember: what goes around comes around.

I am perfect, whole and complete. My world is in sublime order and my life is divinely guided. There is no confusion in my life, because that which has created me is never confused. I am the greatest thing God (or whomever you believe in) has ever conceived.

I have more _____ than I will ever need and I am achieving my goals because I have complete and total happiness. (fill in the blank)

The confirmation you see above is an example of Creative Vision. See the concept? Believing you're the best thing on this earth is not conceit, it's self-esteem. Of course you can't verbalize such a confirmation to other people (they'll feel you're being superior), but you should always *think* that way to yourself. The more you believe in your worth, the more worthwhile your life will become. Your relationships will have more value and the wonderful things you believe you already have will come to you.

Creative Vision Part 2: Planting Love Seeds. An old but wise expression says: you reap what you sow. This is a principle that is also known as *cause and effect*. The belief: whatever you send out into the universe will return to you with mathematical precision.

If you were to plant pumpkin seeds in a pot for example, you wouldn't worry about what will grow. You must realize then, that the same approach can apply to love and achievement. If you plant seeds of love, only love can spring forth and blossom. You plant love seeds by engaging in positive actions for yourself and with other people. Once you've planted the seeds of love, you no longer have to wonder what will materialize in your life. Weeds will grow only when you neglect to cultivate what you've planted by thinking negatively and losing your faith.

Planting seeds of negativity involves expecting the worst from situations and engaging in wrong actions. Wrong actions are those which involve intentionally hurting other people, letting your fears control you, ignoring your inner voice and refusing to accept divine guidance. When you meet a new man for example, and you approach the situation with negative expectations, you increase your chances of having a negative result. As long as you think negatively, you will not obtain your desires and you will feel unhappiness in your life.

There are ways to combat fear and negativity. First, you must identify those beliefs which are harmful to you and then confront them. This will take a lot of courage and can be very difficult. Ask yourself: why do I believe these things that are making me unhappy? Where did these beliefs come from and why do I hold onto them? How can I release these fears and beliefs? What can I do to think more positively?

Identifying your fears and negative beliefs can involve a life review: reflections of your childhood or a traumatic experience in your life, negative people you've known who have hurt or influenced you, fears you have no explanation for, etc. Some women are so unhappy, they need the help of a doctor or therapist to come to terms with damaging beliefs and emotions. If you feel you cannot conquer your fears and negative beliefs alone, you should not hesitate to seek outside help.

Creative Vision Part 3: Thought Control. Controlling your thoughts can help you to eliminate fears and negative beliefs. The way to control your thoughts is to be aware of *how* you're thinking at a given time and consciously make corrections. This type of thought control is referred to as *metacognizance*. On the next page are common negative ideas and improved perceptions. See if any of the negative ideas are familiar.

Destructive Negative Thought

I have the worst luck.

I always manage to attract the wrong men.

Why does this keep happening to me?

Why do men keep doing these things to me?

That was a bad decision I made.

Improved Positive Perception

I've been presented with difficult challenges that I must work to overcome. I'm receiving a life lesson and must stay open to learning.

No matter who I attract, I can choose the type of man I want to be with.

Good and bad things happen to everybody. I can deal with my ups and downs and work harder to maintain my happiness.

The men I've dealt with will do lousy things to every woman. It's not my fault they're idiots, but I need to examine my motivation for choosing them.

There's no such thing as a bad decision. The decision I've made will produce positive growth, despite its initial outcome.

I can't do this. It's too difficult.

I haven't been able to do this YET. But, I refuse to give up. If I keep trying, I will eventually accomplish my goal.

I cannot change my shortcomings.

I know I'll never be perfect, but I can work to improve myself and become the best that I can be.

There are no good men around.

There are good men out there who are worthy of my love, I just haven't met the right one YET. If I make wiser choices, I will be happier in my relationships.

I'll never find a man to love me.

I'm worthy of love and I am selective. I haven't found the right man who is worthy of MY love. I know I deserve the best and refuse to settle for less.

No matter what I do, my life will be the same.

My life will change as soon as I take an active role in changing it. I can do or become whatever I want. I believe in myself.

Creative Vision Part 4: Mind over matter. As you begin to control your thoughts, you will gain greater command of your mind and emotions. You can also increase your psychic abilities and become much more in tune with the universe. Mind over matter involves:

- Learning to stay calm and control anger.
- Hearing and listening to your inner voice.
- Increasing your awareness and sensitivity to the surrounding environment.

Mind over matter can be attained through the development of greater concentration. Concentration is also a door which leads to enlightenment. The key to opening the door is relaxation. The following meditation exercise can help you to relax and concentrate.

Open a window so that you can inhale fresh air. Seat yourself nearby in a comfortable position and place a fresh vase of eucalyptus by your side. Close your eyes. Begin breathing deeply and rhythmically, counting to one hundred. Try to clear your mind of all thoughts. Focus on the noises which surround you and then begin to tune them out, one by one.

When your mind is in complete silence, imagine drifting upon the surface of a clear, tranquil ocean. The water is warm and the waves are rocking your body gently. Floating...

Allow yourself to sink just beneath the surface of the water and remain there suspended. Think about how calm you feel. You're at peace and experiencing renewed feelings of hope and joy. At this point, you can begin your Creative Vision or turn your attention to any other matter which concerns you. The solutions and answers you seek may miraculously appear.

For more on mind over matter read:

Awakening Your Psychic Powers, An Edgar Cayce Guide by Henry Reed, PHD., St. Martin's Press. ISBN: 0-312-95868-4.

Tapping Into The Power by Ayanla Vanzant.

Another Page in my Personal Chapter...

There is no limit to what your mind can produce. Log your thoughts. Suggestions: How can I benefit from what I've read? How do I utilize what I now know? Where do I see myself headed? What are the key points I need to remember?

_____

_____

_____

_____

_____

_____

_____

_____

_____

_____

_____

_____

_____

_____

_____

This is YOUR personal page. Write on! ✎ *More space on the reverse...*

Part Two

Erotica

When Pleasure
Becomes the Principle...

Are You Kinky?

Take this kinky inquiry to find out how you score on the *Delilah Power!* Kinkometer.

Write:	If you feel the statement is...
A	Always true and I like it that way!
B	Sometimes true, to each his own.
C	Okay, I admit it, but don't judge me.
D	Might try it, don't know if I'd like it.
E	Are you NUTS?!!!

To accurately assess your kinkiness, you should respond to all statements candidly. At the end of this section are directions for figuring out and interpreting your score.

A Delilah Power! Kinky Inquiry

1] I like it when a man spanks me. _____
2] Sex is better when it's wild and freaky. _____
3] I like to be submissive, let a man dominate me. _____
4] I gotta have it doggie-style. _____
5] I'm into all positions, depending on my mood. _____
6] I'd like to spank a man when he's naughty. _____
7] I like to get on top every chance I get. _____
8] I play with my man's anus and give rim jobs. _____
9] I love giving oral sex, it makes me climax. _____

10] I prefer to be dominant & make a man behave. _____

11] If a man wants me, he'd better eat me first. _____

12] I like tying up or otherwise restraining a man. _____

13] I get off hurting a man during sex. _____

14] I get turned on by male exotic dancers. _____

15] I often fantasize about sex with strange men. _____

16] I fantasize about having sex with two men. _____

17] I'd like to seduce a young boy (or have already). _____

18] I like wearing erotic clothes for a man. _____

19} I use sex toys for making love & masturbating. _____

20] I have no inhibitions about my body. _____

21] When making love, I like to use dirty language. _____

22] Anal sex really gets me off. _____

23] I like being handcuffed and tied up. _____

24] I like to do it with animals. _____

25] I'm into golden showers and defecation. _____

26) I'm a vampire and like to draw blood. _____

27] I like to do it with women as well as men. _____

28] I don't mind if a man calls me a freak. _____

29] The missionary position is the only one I like. _____

30] I find sex distasteful, prefer not to do it. _____

31] I feel awkward talking during sex. _____

32] I always keep my eyes closed during sex. _____

33] Sometimes I feel ashamed/dirty after sex. _____

34] I'm excited by erotic films and porno movies. _____

35] I like having mirrors in view of the bed. _____

36] I like to make love in public places. _____

37] I like to watch a man's penis enter me. _____

38] I'd enjoy seeing my man screw another woman. _____

39] I fantasize about being raped. _____

40] I'm so horny, I wear every man out. _____

Now, turn to the next page to find out your score...

Erotica

Questions 1-28	Questions 29-33	Questions 34-40
A = 5 points	A = 1 point	A = 5 points
B = 4 points	B = 2 points	B = 4 points
C = 3 points	C = 3 points	C = 3 points
D = 2 points	D = 4 points	D = 2 points
E = 1 point	E = 5 points	E = 1 point

 Now, add up your points.

60-80 points: Your low score indicates you may be conservative to an extreme and engage in sexual activity strictly for procreation. There's also a chance you may be sexually repressed. If you dream of a better sex life, you can achieve one by learning more about your body and how to please it. Try reading the chapter, *To Touch Thyself* for assistance.

80-100 points: Your morals are clearly defined and you are selective with men. Although you appear to enjoy sex, it's probably not the earth-shattering encounter you wish it could be. You might find greater pleasure if you open yourself to new experiences. *The Sweet Flavor of Love* may help you to uncover more of your lovemaking potential.

100-125 points: Although reserved at times, you have a wanton streak that can please the right man. You like to experiment with kinkiness occasionally, but have firm limits. You may also have inhibitions which prevent you from letting go and fully enjoying an erotic experience. *To Touch Thyself.* may give you the inspiration you need to break free.

125-150 points: You have a strong sex drive and a healthy balance of reticence and kink. You're comfortable with your sexuality and probably know how to please a man and control your own orgasms. The entire chapter *Erotica* is tailored for you. Explore the passion and enjoy!

150-175 points: You're certifiably kinky and much freer sexually than most women. You enjoy raunchy variations of the norm. Men find you exiting, but may hesitate to establish a solid relationship with you. Make sure you protect yourself and your partner(s) by using condoms at all times.

175-200 points: You have achieved the highest ranking on the kinkometer and earned the title: *Freak of the Century.* You know no boundaries, are wanton and probably addicted to sex. If you're smart, you protect yourself at all times with condoms *and* spermicide to avoid AIDS and STD's.

If you consider yourself a bold and audacious gal, you'll really appreciate the following books by author, The Righteous Mother:

Get on Top! A Sister's Guide to Life, Love and her Biggest Difficulty... (ISBN: 0-9652540-2-X)

Sit on It! The Pocket Companion to Get on Top! (ISBN: 0-9652540-6-2)

Sex Her Right! A Brother's Guide to the Most Intimate Details. (ISBN: 0-9652540-3-8)

Published by Swing Street. See order forms at the end of this book for more information. Or, log onto Swing Street's website at: **www.goswingstreet.com**.

Related Resources/ Websites of Interest

The Male Sexual Machine by Kenneth Purvis, M.D., St. Martin's Press. ISBN: 0-312-07031-4.

The New Male Sexuality by Bernie Zilbergeld, Ph.D., Bantam Books. ISBN: 0-553-08253-1.

www.aja.com (Ask Jeeves) Log on to ask a question literally about anything. Links to reliable information sources and more.

www.onhealth.com (OnHealth) health/women's issues, including emergency contraception. Links to related sites.

www.whapmag.com (Whap! Magazine) Cool site for those aiming to control a man with female domination and discipline.

Quote of the day: "Sex on T.V. can't hurt you unless you fall off."

The Sweet Flavor of Love
Using Food as an Aphrodisiac

 Did you know...
a man has over 10,000 taste buds?

Wow! That means there's room for a lot of stimulation in his mouth. You should therefore put things in a man's mouth that he will savor, relish and devour! You don't want him to pick, you want him to eat it all!

They say a man is only as good as his last meal. If this is true, then you've got to feed your man the foods that will make him a tiger. Why? because tigers love meat, and yours is the sweetest tasting around.

In this section, you'll discover ways to tickle your man's taste buds, arouse his appetite and satisfy his lustful cravings. He'll be so enamored by you, he'll gladly eat whatever you tell him to. If you'd like to try your hand in the kitchen, you'll enjoy preparing and serving the easy and delightful recipes you'll find. Other delicious formulas for romance are nestled between the remaining chapters of this book, so grab your apron and your garters, pull out the sugar and the sex toys and do your thang! It's time to get saucy!

Gland Talk

The pituitary gland, which is located at the base of the brain, produces hormones that affect growth. This gland is very important because it can make or break your sex life. Researchers have found a strong link between the pituitary gland and sexual activity. In men, the basophil cells of the anterior pituitary gland are directly related to the production of testosterone and sperm and may also affect penis size. Penis size is of definite concern for many of us. Your objective: ensure your man has a healthy pituitary gland. Thus, the following equation:

> *Healthy Pituitary Gland =*
> *Healthy (Hopefully Big and Hard) Penis =*
> *Incredible Sex and Happy Feelings!*

The thyroid gland can also affect sexual performance because of its control over the metabolism. Do you want a lackluster man without energy? What about a man that goes so fast, he ejaculates before you know what hit you? You want him at the right pace, for the right length of time. You want to be satisfied!

The adrenal glands, located above each kidney are what stimulate a man to action when he's excited, afraid, etc. So, when a male gets really hot and horny, you can be sure his adrenal glands are at work. Healthy adrenals give a man lots of energy which in turn, can be great for you. You want his blood pumping and his heart racing, his engine charged and ready to go!

So, what does all this talk about glands mean to you? Knowing a little about the effects of certain foods on a man's glands can mean a great deal when you begin creating aphrodisiacs. The foods you feed a man can make him a better lover. Or, they can make him worse. After reading this chapter, you'll be able to cook up something to make him deliver!

Men often eat foods which decrease their sexual prowess, ignoring those that can turn them into sex champions. In the game of love, a sex champion is a winner. So, let's look at food items believed to stimulate the glands and act as sex enhancers. Then, we'll talk about foods to avoid. As a rule, food items which ensure gastronomical serenity also promote a healthy sex life. But remember, a well-balanced diet is the best way to increase both sex appeal and sexual performance.

Gland-Stimulating, Sex Enhancers

Vitamin A and B-Complex
Champagne
Cider
Chocolate and Cocoa (hot)
Cinnamon, Cloves, Ginger*
Cod liver oil or other fish oils
Cow's liver and Kidney
Curry
Dark beer (in small quantities)
Figs**
Garlic
Gentian
Ginseng Tea and Jasmine Tea
Kola
Mint
Nutmeg
Sea Moss (in milkshake form) and Sea Farine
Shellfish
Whole grain breads and cereals
Zinc

Potential Sex Destroyers

Nicotine
Caffeine
Camphor
Excessive amounts of starch
Overindulgence in sugar
Fatty foods
Salty foods
Overly spiced foods

**Throughout the ages, figs have been held in high regard for their power to create sexual excitement. *Ginger has long been considered a sexual tonic and is rich in protein and anti-oxidants.

Nicotine and caffeine should be ingested in small quantities because they wreak havoc on the nervous system. Too much starch and sugar in the diet can cause obesity and loss of power. Fatty foods, such as fried foods and foods with too much butter and gravy, increase the risk of high serum cholesterol and heart disease as well as make a man lazy. High salt in his diet can cause hypertension. Finally, overly spiced foods can give him bad breath and a lethal case of the farts. In short, he will not be a man with sexual power.

Excessive amounts of strong alcoholic beverages should also be avoided. For a healthy and refreshing addition to your meals, try serving virgin cocktails, apple cider, or a light wine.

Creating the Consistency for Love

When you feel ready for love, it's frustrating to hear a man say he's too tired or stressed out. Although there are occasions when a man just isn't in the mood and should be left alone, he will at other times appreciate being stimulated to sexual desire. If you want sex, but are unsure of how the man feels, observe him as he comes through the door. Are his eyes bright? Does he has spring in his step? Or, does he appear listless and run down? Is he tense? Remember this simple rule for getting him where you want him:

- Warm foods and beverages will relax him.

- Cold foods and beverages will revitalize him.

Don't serve coffee to a man who's "bouncing off the walls" because he'll end up driving you crazy. On the other hand, avoid serving mixed drinks and heavy food to a man who lacks vitality. Use your sensual intuition to choose a food that will improve his outlook and synchronize his energies with your own.

Recipe for Romance #1: Teasing His Tongue

Baby oil
A spoon of brown sugar moistened with water
A blindfold
A small tray or plate
Your favorite fruit liqueur (see: "Know Your Liqueurs")
A small glass
A strawberry
A fresh-cut rose
Your breast

Preparation:

Place the strawberry, rose and spoon with brown sugar on the tray, out of sight. Position the fruit liqueur, oil and glass near your sofa. Wear an attractive garment that allows easy access to your bosom.

When the man is in a receptive mood (neither hungry nor tired), ask him to participate in a secret experiment after which he will receive a huge reward. Say you're testing an hypothesis on taste, texture and consistency (with a seductive smile and mischievous gleam in your eye). He must be completely cooperative, or the experiment will fail. When he agrees, ask him to recline comfortably on the sofa.

Kneel before him and slowly remove his shoes and socks. Maintain eye contact. Pour a small amount of oil into your hands and massage his feet gently, working your way from the toes, to his ankles. When you feel the tension leave his body, put the oil aside and pour a small amount of liqueur into the glass. Have him savor the liqueur slowly, describing the taste in detail. Then, he closes his eyes. Ask how the liquid feels against his tongue. Is it warm and silky? Does he feel it traveling through his body?

Next, blindfold him and retrieve your tray. He cannot use his hands, or touch you in any way. Begin with the strawberry, which is grainy. Have him stick out his tongue. Slide the berry gently against his tongue and lips, encouraging him to describe all sensations. Graze the fruit against his face and neck, asking him how it feels. By now, he may already be excited and want to devour you, but don't let him. Toy with him for a while. After a moment, you can ask him to bite into the fruit and eat it.

Next, you'll use the rose, which is smooth. Have him close his mouth and relax his lips. Be sure to praise him for his efforts. Brush the flower against his lips, cheeks and eyelids. Tickle his ears. Ask him to lick the petals and focus on the texture. How is it different from the strawberry? What does it remind him of? How does it make him feel? Trail the rose over his shoulders, across his chest, between his thighs and down to his feet, making sure to linger in the area(s) which excites him the most. Titillate him by stroking the soles of his feet.

The last item you serve will undoubtedly be the most delicious. Quietly remove your breast and coat the nipple with the brown sugar. Tell him he can only lick the item and not bite it. While he's wondering what you're planning to feed him, insert your sugar-coated nipple into his mouth. The rest will come naturally and he'll soon realize what the reward is!

Recipe for Romance # 2: Playing the Role

Choose one of the exciting recipes at the end of this chapter and surprise your lover by serving him dressed as a waitress: a sexy, horny, ready to be laid-on-the-counter-and-screwed waitress. You can either rent a costume or make one yourself. To make a costume yourself, all you'll need is the following:

A low cut, sexy black top
A short, tight black skirt
A white apron tied at the waist
Black stockings and garter (garter visible beneath hem-line)
A tray
A small notepad
A new perfume fragrance

If you're serving your husband, you can greet him at the door in your costume when he comes in from work. Or, you can sneak off and change when he least expects it. Either way, you'll have his undivided attention. Address him as "Sir", and introduce yourself by another name. Pretend you've never met him before, but find him incredibly attractive.

As you tell him what's on the menu, stand close so he can smell your wonderful, new fragrance. Flirt with him. You can ask him if he's married or has a girlfriend and say you hope he's got a nice, big "tip" to give you. Let him know how good he looks and how much he turns you on. Admiration is a real aphrodisiac for a man.

If you're feeling really naughty, lose the panties. As you bustle around, waiting on him, you can let him in on the secret by dropping a napkin and bending over to retrieve it. Don't be surprised if you *never* finish serving the dish.

Recipe for Romance #3: *Making that Banana Split*

A big, firm banana halved lengthwise
Vanilla ice cream fully softened in the refrigerator
Chocolate syrup
Assorted sprinkles or maraschino cherries
A plastic mattress cover
An inexpensive fitted sheet
4 silk scarves

There's nothing a man loves more than an uninhibited woman in bed for she is unpredictable and exciting. You can totally wow your lover by turning him into your own personal dessert and eating him at your leisure.

Prepare your body and your bedroom in true seductress fashion: the right candles, incense and mystical oils to set the stage for love. Utilize all that you've learned in *Exotica* to create the aura of enticement. When the mood is complete, invite the male into your lair.

After protecting the bed with your mattress cover and sheet, have the man enter the room and lie down. If you can, use silk scarves to loosely restrain his hands and feet against the bed. Stand over him and drop the cold ice cream onto his body by the spoonfuls. Continue to "prepare" your dessert with the other ingredients in the manner you choose.

Once you've split the banana, your man will top it off by adding his own nuts!

Note: If you don't like bananas, try crushed pineapple instead. You can also substitute the other ingredients listed and make an ice-cream sandwich, sundae, etc. Bon Apetit!

Know your Liqueurs

 Liqueurs can be added to coffee and other beverages, drizzled over desserts and cooked with numerous foods. When preparing a dish with alcohol, keep in mind: according to the U.S. Agriculture Research Service (ARS), 40% of alcohol can remain in food after 15 minutes of cooking, 25% may remain after an hour and 10% remains after 2 hours. Alcoholic beverages also contain a high amount of sodium.

Amaretto: almond & apricot-flavored liqueur from Italy
Anise: anise or licorice-flavored liqueur
Applejack: apple brandy
Calvados: French apple brandy
Chambord: black raspberry-flavored liqueur
Cointreau: orange-flavored French liqueur
Creme de cassis: black currant-flavored liqueur
Creme de menth: clear or green mint-flavored liqueur
Curacao: orange-flavored liqueur with a blue color
Galliano: tropical-flavored liqueur from Italy
Godiva: chocolate-flavored liqueur
Goldschlager: cinnamon-flavored liqueur with gold leaf
Grand Marnier: orange-flavored, cognac-based liqueur
Kahlua: coffee-flavored liqueur from Mexico
Kapali: Mexican coffee-flavored liqueur
Leroux: melon-flavored liqueur
Midori: green melon-flavored liqueur
Missar: peach-amaretto liqueur from Italy
Peter Heering: cherry-flavored liqueur from Denmark
Peachtree Schnapps: peach-flavored liqueur
Tia Maria: coffee-flavored liqueur from Jamaica
Triple Sec: orange-flavored liqueur

Beefcake to Go: Filling Up on Fast Food Romances

What is *Beefcake to Go*?

Beefcake to Go is the term I use for fast-food romances: a special kind of man and sex that's quick, cheap, easy, and available everywhere. *Beefcake to Go* is filling at the moment, but not very nutritious emotionally. Men who are *Beefcake to Go* can be mouth watering delights, but they'll probably have trouble leaving a positive and meaningful impression. In other words, they're fun, but they're not worth an emotional investment.

For the rest of this section, we'll be referring to men, relationships, sex and romance in culinary terms. If after reading this you develop an appetite, make your own decisions on what you want to eat and gorge yourself until you're satisfied!

When is *Beefcake to Go* ideal? *Beefcake to Go* is ideal for the hungry Sister when:

- You've got a craving, but don't want to spend a lot of time preparing a "meal".
- You're too busy to eat a full-course dinner.
- You need a snack because the food you *really* want to eat is unavailable.
- You want a hassle-free treat.
- You're simply bored with home-cooked meals and want something different.
- It's your birthday and you want to give yourself a little present.
- You've got that "eat and run" mentality.

While *Beefcake to Go* can certainly satisfy your taste buds, it can have a lot of additives and also ruin a healthy diet. Make sure you're in tip-top shape before you partake. You know you're getting a whiff of some *Beefcake to Go* when:

- The beefcake says there's a female manager or owner supervising the restaurant, but you can get take-out after hours.
- The advertising is false. For example, you get a promise for a "Supersize" meal and a special deal, but the toy in the happy meal is little, or the food is just plain lousy.
- *The Beefcake to Go* has over one million served.
- He tries to serve you junk food on the first date.
- The *Beefcake to Go* is stingy with the bread.

We all have our own tastes in food and no one's in a position to judge. However, if you choose a fast-food romance over one that is longer lasting, keep in mind:

- You can sustain yourself on fast-food indefinitely, but after a while, it may take a toll on your nervous system.
- A well-prepared meal tastes better and provides you with plenty of leftovers.
- As *Beefcake to Go* is available on just about every street corner, choose it carefully. Is it clean? Does it have decent ingredients? Make sure the food is not stale, rotten or infested.
- Always evaluate a meal before you eat it. Where's the cheeze? Does it have "the cheddar" to get you to a real restaurant?
- Most important of all, don't get sick off of *Beefcake to Go*. To avoid an upset stomach and more serious physical complications, fully protect yourself. Always wrap *Beefcake to Go* in latex from start to finish.

Big Banana Bread ™

If you're feening for "The Big Banana", try making this delicious and nutritious bread!

2½ cups all-purpose flour
1 teaspoon salt
2 teaspoons baking powder
½ teaspoon baking soda
1 teaspoon vanilla extract
½ teaspoon ground cinnamon
¼ teaspoon ground nutmeg
1 cup softened butter or vegetable shortening
2 cups sugar (substitute 1 cup brown sugar, if desired)
2 cups mashed ripe banana (roughly 6 bananas)*
4 eggs, beaten
½ cup chopped walnuts (if desired)
½ cup raisins (if desired)
Extra Healthy: Add 1 cup whole bran cereal

Preheat oven to 325°. Lightly grease and flour a 9 by 5-inch loaf pan. In a medium-sized bowl, mix together flour, salt, baking powder, baking soda, cinnamon and nutmeg. In a larger bowl, beat together the butter, sugar, banana, egg and vanilla. Add the dry ingredients and stir until the batter is well blended. Last, mix in the raisins and walnuts.

Pour into pan. Bake for 60-70 minutes. Check for doneness by inserting a knife in the center of the cake. Knife should come out clean. Remove bread from oven and allow to sit for 5 minutes before turning onto a rack. Cool completely before serving. Serves 8-10.

*Prepare banana for mashing by rolling it with your hands against a hard surface. Think about your man. Banana should be tender, supple and warm to the touch before peeling. Power Rating: ☆☆☆

Sleazy Tease me Cheese Cake™

This cake is so delicious, your man will want to eat the whole thing. Give him a small slice because you have something else you want him to eat when he's done!

24 ounces softened cream cheese
1 pint sour cream
½ pint heavy cream
4 eggs, beaten until foamy
⅔ cups flour, sifted
1¼ cups sugar
2 teaspoons lemon juice
3 tablespoons vanilla extract
Crust: 1 stick butter or margarine, softened
½ box vanilla wafers (about 40 wafers)
A slip-joint pan

Preheat oven to 375 degrees. Mix cream cheese, sour cream, heavy cream, eggs, sugar, lemon juice and vanilla in large bowl until well blended. Sift in flour and beat at high speed for about a minute. Place batter in refrigerator.

Put vanilla wafers in a paper bag and crush thoroughly. Toss wafer crumbs with softened butter in a medium-sized bowl until crumbs are fully coated. Press ¾ of the crumb mixture firmly and evenly into the bottom of the pan. Press the remaining mixture around the sides of the pan.

Pour the cake batter into the pan, making sure slip joint is tightly locked.

Bake at 375 degrees for 20 minutes. Turn oven down to 325 degrees and bake for an additional 45-60 minutes or until top of cake is golden brown.

Allow the cake to sit in the pan for at least an hour before opening the slip joint. If using whipped cream cheese, chill cake in refrigerator after initial cooling time, keeping pan intact. Refrigerate 2-3 hours before serving. Rating: ☆☆☆☆☆

Friction & Fiction
Making Love Meet Your Sexpectations

Someone once said great sex is a combination of friction and fiction: mind and body. When a woman joins herself sexually with a man, he ignites the flesh because the *brain* is excited. Now that you have *Delilah Power!* you can make love meet your sexpectations. You can enjoy unparalleled fiction and treat yourself to some hot and heavy friction.

Sex is Life

It's perfectly healthy and natural to love sex. Our creator made sex pleasurable so that human beings will want to procreate and survive as a species. Through sex, one aligns oneself with life.

Throughout history, women have been the ones to control sex. In ancient times, women were worshiped as goddesses, some were able to destroy empires and make conquerors weak with desire. In some cultures, the courtesan, the woman most experienced in the art of making love, was most desired for marriage. From early on, she was trained to please and she knew what to do to keep a man coming back for more.

Even in modern times, sexy women are used to sell everything from cars to frozen dinners. A woman has a natural power to subdue and mesmerize. There's one thing she should always remember however: an easy woman is *never* the one with power, it is instead the female who understands male psychology, the one who uses her brain to cause infatuation and obsession, that's most powerful. As a woman, you have the ability to use and enjoy sex to its fullest. Why not utilize the advantages you have?

There are many ways you can please a man in bed and sometimes, what's unconventional is ultimately more rewarding. Penile-vaginal intercourse is only a small piece of an intricate puzzle. The way you touch a man, the places you kiss and the things you say complete the entire picture. If you're willing to learn and receptive, you can give and receive the most cherished expression of love in unique ways. And when love is the motivation for sex, the joining evokes more than simple pleasure, one attains a feeling of pure bliss.

The Touch Effect

Sensual touching can be a wonderful part of your intimate relationship, a meaningful way to encourage passion, communicate feelings and satisfy your need to be loved. When a man explores a woman with sensual touch, he makes her feel desirable and important. When she touches him in return, he feels appreciated and powerful. Through touch, you can connect emotionally and spiritually with a man, solidifying your relationship.

When touching a man sensually, view his entire body as an erogenous zone. You can stimulate him to lusty action using the tips of your fingers, knuckles or nails (gently, of course). In addition the usual exciting places, you'll find it most effective to rub, caress, stroke and graze:

The backs of his knees
Web spaces between his fingers and toes
The small of his back
His armpits
Behind his ears
The hollow of his throat

You can also take turns touching and being touched. A nice way to touch each other simultaneously is to lie together face to face, or in the 69 position. Create an understanding that each person will indicate when something feels good or unpleasant. Each partner must relax and feel free to experiment. As the man explores you with his hands, pay close attention to how you like to be touched. Close your eyes and concentrate on the sensations you feel. When it's your turn to touch, ask him to describe what he experiences.

Sensual Massage

Sensual massage is an intense form of touching that involves applying more pressure with the hands and concentrating on the muscles. In addition to relieving stress and tension, massage helps the body detoxify itself by getting rid of lactic acid in the muscles and improving circulation, preparing it for rigorous activity. In other words, a great massage can get both you and your man ready for even greater sex!

Eucalyptus, kiwi and jojoba oils are excellent choices for a massage, but virtually any oil will do. Have the man lie on his stomach with his arms at his side. Straddle him lightly, his buttocks beneath your hips. Let him relax his legs and avoid placing too much of your weight on him.

Rub your hands together to create warmth and begin at the small of his back. Press both palms firmly into his lower back and push upward, allowing skin and muscle to slide beneath your hands. Feel for knots and tight spots in the muscles. If you encounter any, apply firm pressure with your fingers and massage the area(s) in a small circular motion. When your hands arrive at his neck, curl your fingers over his shoulders and bring your stroke outward, over the biceps. Bring your hands beneath his armpits and slide them down his sides to their original position above his hips. This "M-shaped" motion should be repeated until his flesh is warm and he appears totally relaxed.

Once he is pliant, massage his calves, hamstrings and chocolate-brown buttocks. Enjoy making those buns hot and greasy. Use your fingers to tickle his spine and smack his rump a few times to show him who's the boss. Turn him over and stroke his temples. Rub his tummy and tickle his thighs. Massage him everywhere he feels tense and he will stiffen uncontrollably in one sweet, delightful area.

Note: To really invigorate him, follow the massage up with a witch hazel rubdown.

The Squeeze Play

There's nothing a man loves more than a hot, tight coochie. Why? Because a hot, tight coochie works his body, clears his mind and restores his equilibrium. Like dust in a vacuum, he gets sucked in and blown away! When your man deserves a reward for good behavior, you can give him what he craves by giving him the squeeze play! The pubococcygeus muscle (also known as the PC muscle) extends from your pubic bone to the base of your spine and can be felt inside your vagina. It helps to support your pelvic organs and contracts spasmodically whenever you have an orgasm. The best thing about the PC muscle: you can squeeze it at will, make it jump, dive and ripple, drive your men wild in bed!

First, let's test your PC to see how strong it is:

Test A: While urinating, stop and start the flow several times voluntarily.

Test B: Insert two fingers in the coochie, spread them apart and try to squeeze them together with your muscles.

If your vaginal muscles aren't strong enough to handle these two tests, don't worry; they will be. You can build up the PC as follows: clench (as when you stopped the flow of urine), hold for a few seconds and then release. Do several repetitions, several times a day. This way of working the muscle is often referred to as the Kegel exercise. You can even buy special items to insert in the vagina for resistance when training the PC, in the chapter *To Touch Thyself* is a listing of websites at which you can purchase these items and other sexual equipment. Get that coochie pumping!

When you consciously contract your PC muscle, you cause blood to flow to the area, increasing lubrication. When making love to a man, you can apply pressure in such a way to keep him hard and intensify his climax. Experiment with different positions until you find the one that affords the most control. Once you establish your own special rhythm, there'll be no stopping you!

As he moves inside of you, you can tease his penis by varying your grip: tighten, then release, stroke softly and squeeze hard. Open yourself wide so he can plunge headlong, fold down the hatches and lock him in. Each thing you do will make him gasp with surprise and want you even more. And as you become more adept at working this "love" muscle, you'll experience stronger orgasms yourself and control your own pleasure.

Lip Service

Every man loves lip service. A woman's worshiping mouth on his stiff organ tells him he is king of all he surveys. The penis is a man's emblem of imperial authority. As he watches you perform fellatio, he will nod his royal head, wave his bulging scepter and say to himself: "This is what life is all about." And as long as you bow to him, he will rule with kindness.

What's more, you as his dedicated sexual servant have a huge responsibility. Not only are you obligated to satisfy him, you must also *love* your job. If you perform oral sex on a man and you do not enjoy it, he will sniff it out in the same way a predatory animal senses fear. He will then feel threatened and insecure, resent you for it and make you *pay*.

Of course you won't bestow the honor of a blow job on any and every man. As a general rule, this intimate act should be reserved for the one you love and trust. In addition, keep in mind the fluids he releases during oral sex could put you at risk for AIDS and other STD's.

A penis is very sensitive and delicate. When fellating a man, always be gentle. Treat his member as though it's the most delicious and tender vittles you've ever tasted. Avoid raking teeth and don't suck too hard. Stroke lightly with your tongue and lips, work the foreskin gently with your fingers. Look up at the man and search his passion-glazed eyes with your own to show your adoration and submission. Admire his penis, long for it and love it because it loves you. Most importantly, make sure your mouth remains moist and eager.

If you're uncertain of how to please your man, ask for his help as you go along. What excites one man may bore another. Don't be afraid to experiment, be ready to take directions. If you show a hunger for his flesh and a willingness to learn, he will be a patient teacher.

Lip service works both ways. If you're giving it, you certainly want to receive it in return. The best way to get a man to "face the nation" is to make the kitty cat very appetizing. When a man masters the art of eating coochie and licks you the right way, he increases in value. You'll be so horny, you'll go looking for him in the daytime with a *spotlight!*

Take heed: the average male doesn't like a smelly coochie. He might screw it on a horny day, but he probably won't lick it. Keep your coochie on the menu by drinking lots of water and eating a healthy diet. Avoid douches, sprays, perfumes and suppositories, these can cause irritation. If you maintain good hygiene, you probably won't need to cover any odors. For exciting tips on making yourself sexable, read *From Hair to Lair*.

On the other hand, if your cat is purely funkadelic, you may need to see a doctor. You could have a vaginal infection or some other medical problem, including a sexually transmitted disease. Get yourself checked. Also read *Health Wealth* for more information.

Exploring Fantasies

Your fantasies are your own business, you don't have to justify or explain them to anyone. Sexual fantasies are healthy: they keep the mind sharp and vitalize the imagination. They also make sexual encounters exciting and more rewarding. A woman must be free to explore her fantasies without inhibitions or shame.

To be able to fully enjoy your fantasies, you have to release all negative thoughts and prior programming and be *proud* of your sexuality. It's okay to dream of other men, even if you're married. There's also nothing wrong with fantasizing about doing kinky things. Psychologists say fantasies don't always indicate true desire and most fantasies are never acted upon. If you want to share some of your fantasies with a man, make sure he's a mature and secure partner. Reveal your fantasies selectively, as some are best kept in the closet.

In Search of "O"

Nothing excites a man more than to please the woman he is fucking, seeing her face contort with ecstasy, her body riveting with pleasure. He fucks her for his own sexual gain, but he also has a goal: to give her that thing known as the big "O". The female orgasm is without question, his greatest indicator of manhood, proof of his strength and prowess. Some men are so anxious about the big "O" in fact, they think they can actually *force* it. Do they have a lot to learn!

Unfortunately, the big "O" can be pretty sneaky as we all know. Without really intending to, overzealous, inexperienced and immature men can actually prevent us from achieving orgasm and being completely satisfied in bed. What's a girl to do when she has to weigh her own frustration in one hand against a man's ego in the other? Why or why do we constantly have to fake it?

You don't and shouldn't have to fake the big "O". Each time you fake an orgasm, you make matters worse for yourself the next time around. Some women spend so much time faking orgasms with the same man (years even), it becomes impossible to reveal the truth and they give up hope. If you're guilty of faking orgasms, you have to realize you're a part of the problem. Want to know how you can achieve orgasms each and every time you have sex with absolutely no faking? The answer is beautiful in its simplicity: don't fake it.

There's a tactful way to let a man know you haven't climaxed and show him what to do to get you there, you have to *tell* him what you need and *ask* for what you want in a non-threatening way. Think of it as directing a blind man to his destination. In order for him to really understand you, you must be clear and encouraging. You have to guide him while letting him explore. Say something like: "Honey, what you're doing feels really good and I love it. I was also wondering if you would... I think that would make me cum."

Men are very sensitive about sexual performance, so don't criticize. Reward him with praise each time he hits the spot and be patient. If he suffers from injured pride, he'll eventually recover. Once a man unlocks the door to the big "O", something magical happens. He'll realize your satisfaction is far more important than his ego and he'll do whatever it takes to make you happy.

Mutual Masturbation

Mutual masturbation is a great way to teach a man how to bring you to orgasm. It's also incredibly exciting. By allowing him to watch you please yourself, you give him the opportunity to learn by example. You will also make him wild with desire. Guaranteed. If you're not accustomed to masturbating, you might discover the chapter *To Touch Thyself* is very helpful.

Mutual masturbation is a form of sharing that can bring you and a man closer together. It creates a level of intimacy and trust that can last throughout your relationship. However you choose to explore together, with lights on or off, in silence or with music, both partners must be comfortable and willing to take emotional risks. Watching a man please himself is immensely erotic. By doing so, you learn more about him and can be a more responsive and intuitive lover.

Become a Connoisseur

Making love is an art. Become a connoisseur of love by surrendering yourself to pleasure. Rare oils, balms, exotic fragrances and delicate creams applied to the body can create provocative physical sensations. Be adventurous and sensuous, reject routines and the ordinary. Obtain some wonderful products from: The Kama Sutra Company, 2260 Townsgate Road, Suite 3, Westlake,Village, CA 91361 (800) 778-7921 on log onto: **www.kamasutra.com**. The books listed below are very informative, can help you perfect the art of making love:

Sensual Massage, by Nitya Lacroix, Owl Book. ISBN: 0-8050-1231-1.

The Complete Kama Sutra translated by Alain Danielou, Park Street Press. ISBN: 0-89281-492-6.

The Tao of Sexology: The Book of Infinite Wisdom by Stephen Thomas Chang, published by Tao Longevity. ISBN: 0-942196031.

The Ultimate Sex Book, A Therapist's Guide to Sexual Fulfillment by Anne Hooper. DK Publishing, ISBN: 1-56458-063-6.

Live to Love and Love to Live

Sex is life, but it can also be life threatening. Live life to its fullest and live wisely. Where, when and however you choose to make love, what's most important is that you obtain what you need from the experience and protect yourself so that you live on.

Say No to Raw Sex!

According to an article in *American Legacy* (Fall 1999, Volume 5/Number 3):

☠ African-Americans represented 37% of AIDS cases reported in 1998, but African-Americans make up only 13% of the U.S. population.

☠ It is believed about 1 in 50 African-American men and 1 in 60 African-American women are infected with HIV.

☠ In 1998, 62% of women diagnosed with AIDS were African-American.

☠ In 1998, 63% of babies born with AIDS were African-American.

☠ More African-Americans were reported with AIDS in 1998 than any other racial/ethnic group.

Scared? You should be. Despite all the warnings and recent statistics, many women of color are still allowing men to have unprotected sex with them. As a Black woman, you're at much greater risk for contracting an STD and AIDS. What can you do to reduce that risk?

Always wash yourself with soap before and after sex. Don't hesitate to refuse sex with a man who won't use a condom. Forget about his feelings and *think only of your health.* A moment of passion could destroy your life or kill you. Stock up on condoms, choose your partners carefully and *never* let a man in raw unless you're in a committed relationship and you both have been tested for HIV and other STD's. Most of all, educate yourself!

The Center for Disease Control (CDC) has a website where you can obtain information on health publications, data and statistics, employment, training and educational opportunities: **www.cdc.gov**. Write or call: 1600 Clifton Road, Atlanta, GA 30333 (800) 311-3435.

Another Page in my Personal Chapter...

You are the sexiest creature on this earth. You're vibrant, sensual and ready to be loved. Why not write about it? Suggestions: Pen a sexual fantasy to share with your lover, or enjoy at your personal leisure. Amaze yourself! And him!

_____

_____

_____

_____

_____

_____

_____

_____

_____

_____

_____

_____

_____

_____

_____

This is YOUR personal page. Write on! ✎ *More space on the reverse...*

Secret Powers of Water and
The Sensual Bath

 Water is truly amazing. 80% of the earth's surface is water and water is the only substance on earth found naturally as a liquid, solid and gas. Everything in and essential to your life is in some way dependent upon water. If you've ever had the opportunity to swim in an ocean or pool, soak yourself in a jacuzzi or tub, or otherwise submerge your body in water, you know what it feels like to connect to this incredible and powerful element.

From the moment of your conception, your embryo depended upon water to live, grew and was nourished in a nutrient-rich, water solution. Today, your body is composed of about 70% water, most of it contained within your cells. When you consume water it flows completely through your body to your brain, regulating your temperature and removing waste from your system, amongst other things. Water is the life in and around us, an undeniable force we need to survive.

The Sensual Bath

In addition to sustaining and cleansing the body, water has *secret* powers to explore: powers which can expand the human conscience, intensify emotions and inspire love. With the sensual bath, you'll learn to harness these powers, broaden your mental horizons, release your sensuality, increase your sensitivity to the world around you. By establishing spiritual connection to water and maintaining it in this way, you nurture your soul and spoil yourself. As a result, you can be healthier and feel much happier. You'll also attract more men because men can't resist a spoiled woman.

Before beginning your sensual bath, think about what you want to accomplish during the session. Do you want to feel sexy? Are there things on your mind you need to temporarily forget? Is there some problem to solve or task to prepare for? Or, do you simply want to relax? Say to yourself: *"I'm doing this because I deserve to be spoiled."*

There are three types of sensual baths covered in this chapter, each offers a unique feeling of well-being. As you develop the habit of taking baths, you'll find yourself feeling calmer and contented in your everyday life. You'll also find yourself looking forward to that quiet time when you can soak your beautiful body, tune out the world and be decadently spoiled.

Prepare for your bath by listening to some relaxing music beforehand. The home should be warm and cozy. Have a comfortable robe and slippers ready, or a silky negligee. As you run your bath water, get yourself in the mood by thinking of the things you want that will make you happy and release all negative thoughts. Just so your baths are always safe and fun:

⊛ Avoid hot baths during your menstrual cycle.

⊛ Use bubble baths and soap products sparingly to avoid vaginal irritation.

⊛ Never take a bath when you're extremely tired. You risk drowning if you fall asleep.

⊛ Keep all electrical items away from the bath. An item that's plugged in but turned off is still a dangerous shock hazard.

The Soothing Seduction Bath: when you want a man at your mercy, you must create the aura of enticement. The music you listen to must be sexy (Isley Brothers, Brian McKnight, Joe). Light a red or pink candle and your favorite incense. Place 10 drops of a mystical oil (see: *Oils, Wax and Scents for Love*) in the bath water, as well as a few drops of your favorite perfume. Pour yourself a glass of light wine or champagne to sip as you soak. As you languish, let your mind focus on the man of your desire, let your body absorb the water's energy. Allow the music to filter through your conscience, like a sponge receiving sensual vibrations.

The Return to Nature Mineral Bath: when you're tired of the hustle and bustle and it's time to feel esoteric. Light a white candle. Place a live plant near the tub in plain view. Put on a tape of natural sounds (rain, waves crashing against a shore, birds, leaves rustling) to absorb as you soak. Imagine yourself naked in a tropical rain forest, about to dip in a warm, natural spring. Run your bath water hot and add:

½ cup natural green clay powder
½ cup natural sea salt
½ cup mineral salts or epsom salt
10 drops mineral oil
a natural sea sponge to wash your skin

The Emotional Release Bath: when everybody's stresing you, and the games people play bore you. This bath works best in complete silence, but music is also soothing. The goal of this bath is simple: clear your mind, think of nothing and just relax!

10 drops of pure eucalyptus oil
1 cup epsom salt
Lavender-scented candle

A sensual bath requires some time and preparation and can be taken at any moment of the day. Allow at least an hour, use as much time as you need. If you're not in a hurry, you can precede the bath by vigorously rubbing your body down with a wet loofah sponge coated with an apricot kernel/oatmeal scrub. Make an oatmeal scrub yourself by mixing a half-cup of dry oatmeal with a few tablespoons of warm water. After applying your scrub, shower off lightly and then fill your tub. Another option is to make a thin paste using natural green clay powder or mud, apply it to your entire body and let dry. Slough off the body wrap with a loofah and warm water.

If you've read the chapter *Crystal Clear* and are tapping the powers of crystal energy, you can soak your crystals in the tub with you, cleansing, clearing and programing them at the same time. The crystals will also emit electromagnetic energy into the water, making the bath more sensual. This technique of channeling crystal energy works best with the *Return to Nature Mineral Bath*.

Other great oils to use in the bath are jojoba, sweet almond, mineral oil and Vitamin E oil. Only a few drops will soften the water and soothe your skin.

After your sensual bath, you can unleash the power of suggestion by anointing yourself with a mystical oil or partaking in an aroma remedy. Also investigate the many essential oils that are available in aromatherapy stores. Pamper your skin with an emmolient-rich lotion, dust your cleansed, sensual body with powder and spritz yourself with perfume. Wrap your lovely limbs in your silky robe and complete the experience with a refreshing cup of iced herbal tea or exotic juice. Sit back, relax and say to yourself: *"I've just done this because I deserve to be spoiled."*

The beauty of the sensual bath is that its power is pure in any form. Even soaking in plain hot water will benefit you, for water is the true medium through which you can find yourself. Like your imagination, it has no limits and knows no boundaries. Be creative, be daring, make your baths fun and exciting. Have a man join you in your bath so he can participate in your wonderful experience. Most of all, spoil yourself!

More About Water:

⊛ Water regulates the earth's temperature by acting as an insulator.

⊛ You can live without food for over a month, but you can only last about a week without water.

⊛ Your body needs at least 2½ quarts of water each day from all sources in order to remain healthy.

⊛ You lose about ½ liter of water each day through breathing.

⊛ 75% of your brain is water.

To Touch Thyself

To touch thyself is to explore. . .

To explore thyself is to learn.

To learn oneself is to know.

To know oneself is to love.

To love thyself is to love others. . .

To love others is divine!

To Touch Thyself
Exploring masturbation for self-empowerment and spirituality.

You are the most beautiful thing on this earth, a divine creation. You have your own dreams, thoughts, fears, desires and experiences, all unique and special. No one else could ever be quite like you. How wonderful it is to be original. What a blessed state of being!

Your female body is perfect and exquisite, replete with millions of nerve endings that can give you the sweet rush of physical, emotional and spiritual pleasure. It is your right to want and need that pleasure. It is also a healthy, natural and normal process for a woman.

Masturbation is the sublime act of making love to yourself. It is a pure and wonderful way for you to tune into your body and fulfill your own sexual needs. It is in fact, one of the greatest gifts of love that you can give to yourself. And as you receive, you are completed.

Although sex is a physical act, sexual enjoyment can have a deeply spiritual origin. Through masturbation, a woman is able transcend the confines of her physical body and become whatever she wants to be. She is within herself and without. She is in complete control of her own thoughts and her own body. Like a bird whose wings have caught a powerful wind, she can lift herself up, take flight and soar!

Although a number of women are not comfortable with masturbation (perhaps because we've been taught to repress out sexuality as children), more and more are learning to satisfy themselves and thus receive profoundly rewarding pleasure in sex. There is nothing wrong with touching yourself so that you can have an orgasm. In fact, learning to masturbate may enable you to achieve orgasms of greater intensity when you're with a partner. Many men place female masturbation high on their list of fantasies. For them, it's an extremely erotic experience to see a woman release her inhibitions and please herself. Masturbation is also the safest sex, short of abstinence.

Masturbation can also help you with problem solving. Every woman has moments when she must go within herself to resolve an issue, or tend to a private thought. When you are tense, anxious, upset or confused, the physical release you receive from masturbation can be very therapeutic. Touching yourself, exploring yourself and pleasing yourself are all ways to empower yourself.

If you do not masturbate, but feel you can muster the courage to try something new, why not experiment a little? The more connected you become with your own body, the more satisfied you'll probably be in your sexual relationship with someone else. Why not say this sexual confirmation aloud?

I am comfortable with my sexuality. I love sex and I'm not ashamed of it. I love having orgasms. There's nothing wrong with wanting a man inside of me and I'm not embarrased by my needs.

Now that you've confirmed your sexuality, it's time to open the door to a new form of ecstasy! In this chapter, the process of exploring masturbation has been spread over several days. However, you may wish to proceed at a faster pace. Whatever you decide to do is fine, because it's your body and your orgasms. In other words, it's all about Y-O-U!

Day 1: Courting Yourself

The first step in making love to yourself is to infatuate yourself. Suggestion: buy yourself a beautiful bunch of flowers, the loveliest bouquet you can afford. When you arrange your flowers in a vase at home, think of how much you adore yourself and how loved the blossoms make you feel. Imagine you've hand-picked them from

Erotica

the garden of love, allow yourself to become intoxicated with the delightful fragrances. Place the bouquet by your bedside so that you can see them upon awakening. If you don't already own a personal lubricant, now is a good time to buy one. Using a lubricant during masturbation is recommended, because it won't dry as quickly as saliva. *Astroglide* is an excellent choice, it's very similar to your natural secretions. You can also buy yourself some other "love gift", some wine, champagne, or sexy underwear for example. I suggest flowers because they're beautiful, cheerful and undeniably romantic.

Day 2: Self-Exploration

The morning after buying your flowers, allow yourself extra time for your shower. Prior to showering, warm your body lotion by placing it in a bowl of hot water...

Slowly lather yourself, focusing on the slippery feel of the soap against your skin. Pretend your washcloth is a lover, caressing you gently. Close your eyes and open your mind. Feel the warmth and wetness of the water washing over you, like beautiful rain from heaven, imagine your pores opening hungrily to receive their divine nourishment. Spend time lathering your nipples and vaginal lips, lingering as long as you desire. Release your fears and allow yourself to enjoy it. Breathe slowly and concentrate, relishing every sensation.

When you exit the shower, take a moment to stand in front of a mirror. Forget about the imperfections you *think* you see. Instead, focus on the real you, the woman you are *inside*. Visualize your inner beauty as an apparition surrounding and covering you. Let it envelope you. If you feel an urge to touch yourself, do so, remembering every bit of your flesh is exquisite and deserving of love.

As you dry your body, try to discern the fibers of the towel's fabric. Imagine the terry cloth is covered with tiny hairs tickling your skin. The goal is to heighten your awareness and sensitivity to everything that touches you. Next, take the lotion you've warmed and apply it slowly and lovingly. Let yourself go. Satisfy your skin in the following ways:

Feel the lotion between your fingers.
Caress the lotion lovingly into your breasts.
Stroke your hips and tummy.
Rub your buttocks.
Toy with your navel.
Stroke the backs of your knees.
Tickle the crooks of your arms.
Massage your feet, especially between the toes.

Day 3: Experimentation

Visit a sex shop and purchase a sex toy. You'll find a range of exotic items from which you can choose. For many women, sex toys are fun, exciting and satisfying. Some enjoy using vibrators, others prefer dildos. Some women rely only on their fingers and never play with toys at all. Going into a sex shop can be an uncomfortable experience. If you have trepidations about it, take a girlfriend with you and make it a fun outing. You can also purchase a sex toy in the privacy of your home through mail order or if you have a computer and access to the internet. Websites/sources to explore are:

www.babeland.com (Toys in Babeland) This sex toy shop is run by women for women.

www.goodvibes.com (Good Vibrations) San Francisco retail store and mail order. Call for catalog (415) 974-8990.

Eve's Garden 119 W. 57th Street, NYC 10019 (212) 757-8651.

Day 4: Self-gratification

When you feel ready to make love to yourself, plan a time when you'll be undisturbed. Get sexy for yourself. Put on something that makes you feel desirable and irrestible. Make sure the room is quiet. Decide whether you'll feel comfortable using the sex toy(s) at this point. Also have your lubricant handy.

Lie or sit in any position you choose and focus on relaxing. Your hands should be warm. You can begin by touching your breasts, thighs or lips. If you like, create a wonderful fantasy in your mind. You're with the man of your dreams. Who is it? What would he be doing to you? Imagine your hands are *his* hands. Let them touch you everywhere.

Think of how wonderful an orgasm would feel. Ask yourself what you can do to achieve one. Don't feel silly, don't tell yourself you can't do it. Remember, this is *your* private time and *your* body. You can and should please yourself.

Throughout history, the vagina has been compared with and referred to as a fruit or flower. Imagine you're about to unfold a delicate and tender rose bud. Wet your fingers with saliva, or your personal lubricant. Breathe deeply and relax. Touch the petals (lips) of your rose gently, don't try to force a feeling, simply focus on *what* you're feeling. Use the base of your fingers to caress the sensitive, inner creases of your flower. Lightly touch the bud that is your clitoris and allow it to grow. Continue to stroke yourself gently, letting your mind wander. Imagine your fingers are a tongue, licking you softly.

From this point on, let your body tell you what it wants. Give in to its demands and surrender your heart and spirit. Let the sensations of self love lift you until you're gliding. As you release your fears, your body will begin to coast on a stream of passion. At this moment, all that will matter is what feels good to you. By all means, continue to seek your rightful pleasure.

Orgasms can be very elusive. Don't expect an orgasm to happen immediately, although one certainly can. If your body is not ready to release, don't force it. When it comes to masturbation, practice will make perfect. You may have to try several times before reaching your goal.

If you decide to use a sex toy, be certain the object is clean and lubricated, wash it before and after every use. Be very gentle with yourself. Some women develop minor vaginal infections from frequent and/or excessive masturbation, particularly when placing objects inside the vagina. If you notice any changes in your normal vaginal secretions, or experience prolonged soreness or itching after masturbating, see a doctor or gynecologist immediately.

To Touch Thyself is Divine!

Making love to a man can be a most fulfilling sexual experience, but it's also great to please *yourself*. By not having to rely on someone else to achieve orgasm, you care for your body, worship your spirit and fulfill your own needs. Isn't that what self love is all about?

Related Resources

Are We Having Fun Yet? The Intelligent Woman's Guide to Sex by Marcia Douglass and Lisa Douglass, Hyperion Press.

Ordinary Woman, Extraordinary Sex by Dr. Sandra Scantling and Sue Browder, Dutton, New York.

Sacred Sexuality by A.T. Mann & Jane Lyle, Element Books, Inc. ISBN: 1-85230-658-0.

Sexational Secrets: Exotic Advice Your Mother Never Gave You by Susan Crain Bakos. ISBN: 0-312963416.

Secrets of the Superyoung by David Weeks, ISBN: 0-425172589.

Pussy Cat Peach Cobbler ™

Here, kitty kitty. Do you want your man to purr? Try serving him this delicious peach cobbler for dessert. The aroma will arouse his appetite for you and the taste will make him insatiable. Grrrrr!

6 cups ripened peaches (about 8 fruits)
1½ cups sugar
2 tablespoons lemon juice
1 teaspoon vanilla extract
dash of cinnamon
dash of nutmeg
1½ cups flour
1½ teaspoons baking powder
2 eggs, beaten
½ cup melted butter or margarine
¼ teaspoon almond extract
2 tablespoons brown sugar and ½ teaspoon cinnamon
2-quart baking dish

Preheat oven to 350 degrees. Mix peaches, ½ cup of the sugar, lemon juice, vanilla, dash of nutmeg and cinnamon in a bowl. Transfer to dish and set aside. In another bowl, mix remaining sugar, flour, baking powder, eggs, butter and almond extract. Mix until moist and lumpy. Do not over mix. Spoon batter over peaches. Sprinkle with brown sugar and cinnamon mix. Bake for 40+ minutes or until golden brown. Allow to cool. Makes 8 servings.

Pussy Cat Peach Cobbler goes great with ice cream, milk or whipped cream. I highly recommend using whipped cream. After the man finishes the cobbler, he can make you his own tasty pastry! Rating: ☆☆☆☆☆

White Chocolate Mousse with Whip Appeal ™

When the man deserves to be whipped, this is your mousse. Simple to make and exciting to eat, this dessert teases and pleases. Serve in your nightie with fresh-brewed coffee or espresso. Feed him sensuously. Watch him lick the spoon clean!

6 ounces white chocolate
1½ pints heavy cream
¼ cup confectioners sugar
8 egg whites
1 teaspoon cream of tartar
⅓ cup sugar
½ teaspoon vanilla
4 tablespoons white chocolate liqueur (optional)

Slowly melt chocolate in a double boiler (the same effect is achieved by setting a small pot inside another pot of boiling water). Once the chocolate is melted, beat it vigorously until smooth. Remove from heat and allow to cool. In a separate large bowl, whip heavy cream until stiff peaks form. Add the confectioners sugar gradually and beat for an additional minute. Set aside.

In another large bowl, whip the egg whites with the cream of tartar until foamy. Add the remaining sugar and white chocolate. Add the chocolate liqueur. Beat at high speed for about a minute. Last, fold in the whipped cream and transfer to 6 wine glasses. Chill the mousse for at least 5 hours before serving. Serves 6.

For extra delicious taste, drizzle the mousse lightly with raspberry sauce. Place a chocolate medallion in the center to give your dessert that professional touch. If you're really daring, accompany mousse with spike-heeled leather boots, whip and handcuffs. Rating: ☆☆☆☆

Sexy Aging

"Real women don't have hot flashes, they have power surges."

Getting older has some great advantages. As a mature woman, you understand the game and can choose when and how you'll play it. All that you've worked for in your life begins to culminate in wonderful ways and your perspective of the world and people becomes clearer. Chances are you waste less time with useless individuals, have developed patience and foresight and are secure emotionally. You've gotten to know yourself better and are more in tune with your body. The list of pluses goes on and that's a lot to be happy about.

Unfortunately, we're living in a youth/beauty oriented society which can make it difficult for a woman to appreciate what aging has to offer. Without the proper frame of mind, aging can in fact, be very depressing. Now that you have *Delilah Power!* however, you can ignore society and become a sexy, mature woman: the sexiest you can be. And when you've achieved the ultimate in sexydom, you'll be proud and sexually satisfied!

Let's begin with a little confirmation. Read it to yourself and then again aloud:

I am a mature woman. This is who I am and I'm very excited about it. I'm sexy, vibrant and irresistible. I have a lot to offer and many great experiences await me. I can look forward to what life presents in the coming years because I know life will be wonderful.

A woman of any age can be sexy if she has vibrancy, an appreciation of life and an undying optimism. If she loves men, wants men and needs men, she will always be appealing to men. Sex appeal is something that a woman emanates from within. Without speaking a word, she lets the opposite sex know that she is hot, ripe and ready for the taking. Every man, young and old will recognize and appreciate that.

Revitalize your Sex Appeal

The best way for you to feel sexy is to take loving care of your body and mind. When your life is filled with responsibilities, you can get locked into dreary routines and become bored. After having a number of negative experiences with men, it's easy to lose interest in them altogether. If you're bored and lack interest, it's time for a lifestyle change! Here are a few suggestions:

- ❀ Get a fresh, new hair cut and keep it styled.
- ❀ Spend a day at a spa, getting a complete makeover.
- ❀ Buy some new clothes that are stylish and attractive for your figure.
- ❀ Flirt with men, whether younger or older than you. Flirting is healthy and makes you feel good.
- ❀ Get yourself a younger man... if you dare!
- ❀ Join a gym or spa and pamper yourself regularly.
- ❀ Mingle with your peers, start dating and get involved in social groups.
- ❀ Recharge your sex life with your husband or lover.
- ❀ Let the wonder years last your entire lifetime. Life is an adventure with surprises around every corner!

Sex... The Way it Should Be

For many mature women, sex can be an immensely gratifying experience. Post-menopausal women reportedly have the greatest sex, because they have fewer inhibitions, more awareness of their sexuality and no fear of pregnancy. You can and should have sex if you want to, it's one of the healthiest things you can do for your body, mind and spirit. You deserve to be uplifted!

Get Your Groove On!

- ❀ Explore your body and your fantasies. Masturbate. For more on masturbation, see the section, *To Touch Thyself.*
- ❀ Seduce your husband or lover with a *Recipe for Romance* (See: *The Sweet Flavor of Love*).
- ❀ Rent a Black porno movie and enjoy the show!
- ❀ See an exotic male revue. Or two, or three! Hang out with the girls and watch those lean, hard body young males gyrate to the music and give you a personal show for a dollar. By all means, grab a feel and enjoy what you feel!

And Keep Feeling Sexy!

Reduce your stress. In addition to having a profound effect on physiological and mental health, stress shows on your face and lessens your attractiveness. Cynicism, lack of trust and pessimism also affect appearance.

Take a few moments each day or week to reflect on past events and evaluate what you've accomplished. Gain insight on where you're headed by reviewing your life and pinpointing and addressing unresolved issues.

Value the present and imagine the future. Picture yourself as you would like to be five years from now. How would you describe yourself? What would your life be like? What would you like to accomplish?

Stay younger with religion and meditation. Studies show religious faith may increase longevity because it can help you cope with emotional stresses. Meditation increases control of the mind and body, promotes relaxation and spiritual harmony.

Start articulating and negotiating your needs. Know what you want, express it and then negotiate it. Express what you need in your relationships, from your family and friends and in the workplace. At the same time, keep in mind that compromise can benefit everyone.

Don't live for others. You don't have to live to please anyone but yourself. And you don't have to give any excuses for the choices you've made in your life. Be comfortable with yourself and enjoy who you are, every step of the way. Make every moment in your life count!

Refuse to settle for mediocrity. If it's not the best, then it's not for you. Work to harness your talents, abilities and energies in a positive, sexy manner.

Last but not least, say your confirmation daily. Affirm, reaffirm and be firm about who and what you are: mature, wonderful and sexy!

A World without Justice

There was a man who took great care of his body. He lifted weights, jogged 6 miles a day and tanned himself every weekend. One day, he looked in the mirror and noticed he was completely bronzed, except for his penis. Perturbed, he decided to do something about it. He went to the beach, got naked and buried himself in the sand, leaving his pale penis sticking out.

A few minutes later, two elderly ladies came strolling up the beach, the older one using a cane. Upon seeing the penis, she frowned and began to move it around with the walking stick. After a moment she shook her head, sucked her teeth and turned to her friend.

"There's no justice in this world." she said.

The other lady asked what she meant.

"When I was 20, I was curious about it. When I was 30, I enjoyed it. When I was 40, I asked for it. When I was 50, I paid for it. When I was 60, I prayed for it. When I was 70, I forgot about it. Now, I'm 80, the damn things are growing wild on the beach and I'm too stiff to squat!"

What Mama Says
"Old School" Concepts for True Romance.

A mother can be a girl's best friend. Having lived much longer than you, Mom speaks from experience and advises you with love. My mother is a magnificent woman who raised me both with strong morals and an open mind. Being the hard-headed child that I was, I couldn't appreciate her teachings until I'd taken my share of hard knocks. Looking back, I wish I'd saved myself some heartache by having the sense to recognize her wisdom and trust her judgment.

Whether men are from Mars or some other planet, they can drive women crazy. They can also fill our lives with happiness. My mother schooled me early on men, her observations while general, have proven true on many occasions. Perhaps her teachings can help you to understand the male species better and thus maintain your own sanity. Just remember, every man has his own assortment of great qualities and insufferable idiosyncracies.

What Mama Says about Men and Sex

- ☺ Men are simple creatures with fairly simple needs. Keep them well-sexed, well-fed & well-entertained if you want them to stay well-behaved.

- ☺ Men are erotic creatures. They love to have sex and they fantasize constantly. Pussy is more than a physical thing, they see it as their destiny and a touch of heaven in this mortal life.

- ☺ Men are visual creatures. They want what they see and lust after what they *can't* see.

- ☺ Men are horny. Few men go longer than two weeks without having sex with somebody or *something*.

- ☺ Men love freaky women, but not for marriage.

☺ Some guys are mailmen who want to treat you like a stamp: they want to lick you, stick you and send you on your way. What a special delivery!

☺ Men sometimes lack discretion with sex and will lose caution in a moment of passion. Women are at substantially higher risk for AIDS and STD's. It is *your* job to protect *yourself* by insisting on a condom. No rubber, no lover!

☺ Unless a man is a freak, he usually will perform oral sex only on a woman he trusts and/or adores.

☺ Most men welcome sex from women who'll give it freely and easily. However, once a man sees you as easy, he will resist loving you.

What Mama Says about Men, Love and Relationships

☺ Men are hopeless romantics, idealistic about love. When a man really falls for a woman, he only sees the best part of her. This can make him very easy to seduce and deceive.

☺ The more a man likes you, the less he will discuss you with his peers.

☺ The more a man cares for you, the more he will share intimate parts of his life.

☺ Once a man formulates a negative opinion about you, it will be difficult to change it. Conversely, once a man perceives you favorably, he'll always remember you that way unless you hurt him deeply or betray him.

☺ A man's actions should be taken at face value. If a man treats you poorly, it's because 1) he doesn't care and 2) you are allowing it. You can rationalize his behavior any way you see fit. His actions however, are the solid indication of how he feels.

☺ A man will *always* make time to see you if he genuinely likes you. If a man you're dating suddenly becomes unavailable, give him space. He may care for you more than you suspect and need time to adjust to his new feelings. Don't sweat a man and never track him down. It will turn him off and even scare him.

☹ If a man never tells you he loves you, it's because he probably doesn't. He may like you, but he's not in love. You can't force a man to love you if he doesn't. So, you can either settle for less, or find someone who'll love you the way you deserve.

☺ A man will always put his money where his heart is. If the man you're dating cuts corners with you and spends freely on himself, he's not as interested as he should be. Or, he's extremely selfish. Either way, you're better off without him.

What Mama Says about Male Nature

☺ Men are creatures of habit and will usually stick to a pattern. This makes it easier to detect when they're doing something wrong. If your man changes his pattern, buckle down, increase your surveillance and tighten the leash.

☺ Men are creatures of contradiction. Either they act impulsively or methodically, depending upon their moods. The way to deal with this: be sensitive to your man's moods and use good timing to get what you want. For example, take him shopping for your gift when he's feeling impulsive, ask him to fix something around the house when he's in his methodical mode.

☺ Men require a degree of stability and order in their lives. They need a safe haven to run to after each adventure. All men have a strong den instinct and feel secure in their own private spaces. Be a secure influence in a man's world to secure his trust and affections.

☺ Men are competitive. Notice the fervor with which they watch and compete in sports. When a man feels like a winner, he's completely happy.

☺ Men are "result" driven. This is why they're so obsessed with the female orgasm, luxury cars and other symbols of success.

☺ Men are often confused. This isn't totally their fault, however. Society tells men to be macho one minute and sensitive the next, superstuds and faithful husbands at the same time. It can be very hard for them to know what to be and *when*.

☺ Men are good at holding out. They can last a long time without calling you. When a man gets really angry, forget about concessions. *You'll* have to make the first move. Learn when to stroke his ego.

☺ Men are analytical and meticulous. They also love to measure things. If your man likes to cook, let him. Note the great chefs, who are predominantly male and make wonderful dishes.

☺ Men can be big babies when sick, hungry or tired. This is when they really appreciate some female nurturing.

☹ Men generally take longer to mature emotionally than women, but they reach their sexual peak earlier. When a woman's libido is on the rise, a man's prowess is on the decline. This is why older women tend to adore younger men.

☹ Men are greedy. Some of them are never satisfied with what they have and will self-destruct.

☹ Men can have trouble admitting their faults and mistakes. The reason: their egos won't let them.

☺ Men like to feel in control. This is why some of them seek out passive, submissive females. If you're the *passive-aggressive* type, you can still rule from the backseat. As they say, you don't have to be at the helm in order to steer the boat.

☺ Men need personal space to get into themselves and solve their problems. When a man seems distant or preoccupied, give him space.

☺ Men are more sensitive than they let on. Their fear of being hurt or appearing weak causes them to display false bravado or act uncaringly.

What Mama Says about Righteous Female Behavior

☺ Avoid judging men strictly on esthetics. What looks good on the outside can be very *ugly* on the inside.

☺ Avoid bringing negative views into a new situation. Give each new man a clean slate upon which he can etch his own history. In other words, don't let the ex-man affect the next man.

☺ Set proper boundaries early in the relationship and demand respect. Some men test women to see how much they can get away with. Don't let infatuation or fear of losing a man's interest override good judgment. If you tolerate bad behavior from a man at the outset, you'll *always* be subject to it.

☺ *Always* protect the kitty and your body by using condoms. Never let a man intimidate you into having unprotected sex.

☺ Make your needs clear early on without being controlling or demanding. At the same time, be ready to address the man's own needs.

☺ Be consistent in your behavior. Inconsistency will be interpreted as a sign of weakness.

☹ The monster you create will destroy you in the end. If you spoil a man by catering to his every whim, allowing infidelity in a so-called committed relationship and so on, you are creating a monster. Some women want a man so badly, they'll take one any way they can get him. Others don't mind sharing and would rather have half, or a piece of a man than no man at all. You deserve a whole man who loves you and is willing to commit all of himself. However, if you don't believe you deserve such a man, you'll never find him.

☹ Never try to buy a man. Don't give expensive gifts or money to someone you've begun to date unless your goal is to purchase a gigolo. Although he'll never tell you, the man will perceive you as both desperate and foolish. He won't be committed to you and he'll devote himself to using you.

☹ Beware a man that asks you to loan him money, for any purpose. A man with pride and integrity will *never* ask a woman for money unless she's his wife or woman and they *share all expenses*.

☺ If you decide to entrust a man with a large loan, check him out thoroughly beforehand and get him to promise repayment *in writing*. I know a girl who was scammed out of thousands of dollars by a man later found to be wanted by the FBI. He essentially had sex with her for a few weeks and then swindled her. The man was part of a criminal ring that ran the same scheme on dozens of other women. When you like someone, your inclination will be to trust him. However, no matter how convincing a man seems, he may very well be lying.

☺ Learn to forgive and forget in a new way. Certain actions are inexcusable and indicate a fatal personality flaw. If a man commits unacceptable acts and hurts you, forgive him and then *forget* him!

Part Three

Practica

When Only the Best
is Good Enough...

Money Madness

There's no better time than the present to assess your financial health and take steps to improve it. No matter your level of income, you can benefit from basic financial planning. We all know saving money can be difficult, especially when you have very little and want for a lot. However, the less money you make, the more you should monitor your spending and try to save.

Every dollar you spend or save counts. For example, if you were to put just two dollars a day in a jar for a year, you would end up with over seven hundred dollars saved. That's quite a bit of cash. You could take a vacation with that amount of money, improve your house or apartment, get a serious make-over, or consider investment options. Just imagine what you can accomplish using the same two-dollar-a-day strategy over a three year period!

Where Did all The Money Go?

A sensible move would be to figure out exactly where your money is going. Try keeping a daily record of what you spend above your mandatory bills for two weeks. At the end of this time period, you will probably recognize a pattern. You may also discover you actually waste money on unnecessary things. Take a careful look at your spending and decide what you can live without. Sticking to a budget and saving money requires some discipline. But, you'll sacrifice now so that you and your family can benefit later.

If the thought of creating and sticking to a budget makes you yawn, you're not alone. After paying all those bills, you might not have a lot left over for fun things like shopping, hanging out, etc. If however you can create a sound budget, you may afford to occasionally do the things you want and build up a decent savings account in the process. In short, a little discipline can take you a long way.

The amazing thing about a budget is, it becomes less boring as time goes on. When you begin to see the results of your efforts to save, you will be inspired to save even more. The downside is, you will also be very tempted to spend what you've saved. There is only one way to resist the temptation to spend: Self Control!

What are some good money-saving strategies? Your assignment: Read the suggestions below. Then, turn to page 123 (your personal page) and write down five other strategies you think could save you money.

Create a secret stash. Put two dollars a day in hiding for a month. Tell no one about your stash. Don't touch the money, no matter what. At the end of the month, put the sixty-plus dollars in a savings account and pat yourself on the back. Repeat this strategy month by month for a year. Or, put a fixed amount of money in a savings account every week or every payday, the most you can afford.

Pool resources with other family members. Everyone agrees to contribute a certain amount to a savings account every week or two. Someone who is responsible is placed in charge of the account. Everyone decides upon a goal and the time in which the goal should be achieved.

Plan for large purchases and unforeseen circumstances. Just when you need it the least, you might get hit in the pocketbook: unemployment, illness, family emergencies and more. If you know it's almost time to replace an appliance or pay a large bill, begin stashing money away now. A few dollars tucked aside can cushion a financial blow in the future.

Walk to any destination under a mile and put the money you saved in your secret stash. The benefits are two-fold: You save bucks and burn calories.

What about Investing?

Let's say you've established a budget, stuck to your savings routine and achieved your immediate financial goals. You have anywhere from three to six months living expenses accrued in your stockpile and you realize you actually have excess savings. You may be considering retirement possibilities and/or building an investment portfolio. You may have heard of money market accounts, certificates of deposit (CD's), stocks, mutual funds and bonds, but need clarification of the benefits, drawbacks and differences of these options. What should you do?

Investing money can be a complicated process. It would be wise to talk to a professional about ways to invest so that your money can grow, produce income or both. As there is always risk involved in investing, you want to be well aware of what you're getting into. There are a number of books on the topic of investing, you may want to check out the ones listed below. It may also be helpful to tune into your local financial channel and watch their programs. You may not understand what is going on at first, but you will ultimately learn a great deal. Some shows will allow you to call in and ask questions on the air.

www.fantasystockmarket.com Investor education site gives you $100,000 of fantasy money to trade each month. Definitely a site to check out if you want to learn while you earn.

The Wall Street Journal Guide to Understanding Personal Finance by Kenneth M. Morris and Alan M. Siegel, published by Lightbulb Press, Inc.

The Basics of Investing by Gerald Krefetz, published by Dearborn Financial Publishing.

The First Time Investor: How to Start Safe, Invest Safe & Sleep Well by Larry Chambers and Ken Miller, published by Erwin Professional Publishers.

Where Credit is Due...

One solid step in improving your financial health is to check your credit reports. Even if you do not have any credit cards, you may want to view the information listed under your name just to see what is there. Sometimes, information can appear in a credit report due to error. You need to know what information your personal credit report contains. Your credit report can and will affect you in significant ways, such as when you want to obtain insurance and employment, finance a house or buy a new car. A good credit rating increases your buying power and can make life a lot easier.

The three credit reporting agencies listed in this section are the ones most commonly used by creditors. You can obtain a copy of your credit report by calling, writing or visiting their web sites. As of the date of this printing, each agency charges a fee of eight dollars for a personal credit report.

If you applied for credit within the last 60 days and were denied, you are entitled to a free copy of your credit report. If you are unemployed and plan to seek employment within the next 60 days, are receiving public assistance, or believe you are a victim of fraud, you may be able to obtain copies of your credit report without charge. You must submit your request in writing and be able to verify your circumstances.

When writing the credit agencies, you must include your full name, including middle initial and generation such as Jr. or Sr., date of birth, social security number, address and any previous addresses within the past 5 years. If you are not eligible for a free report, include eight dollars payable to each credit reporting agency.

Experian (formerly TRW) (888) 397-3742 P.O. 2104 Allen, TX, 75013-2104 **www.experian.com.**

Trans Union (800) 916-8800 P.O. Box 390 Springfield, PA 19064.

Equifax (800) 755-3502/(888) 978-0146 fax P.O. Box 740256, Atlanta GA, 30374-0256 **www.equifax.com**

If after receiving your credit reports you find errors or omissions, immediately contact all three credit reporting agencies in writing and notify them of the discrepancies. You may also want to check out the following book:

The Guerrilla Guide to Credit Repair: How to Find Out What's Wrong With Your Credit Rating — and How to Fix It. by Todd Bierman and Nathaniel Wice. Published by St. Martin's Press.

If you're in Debt Trouble...

Under the **Fair Debt Collection Practices Act**, it is against the law for a debt collector to:

- Call your place of business in regards to the debt.
- Call you at home before 8 a.m. and after 9 p.m.
- Pretend to be lawyers and threaten legal action.
- Speak to you in a threatening or abusive manner.
- Contact your family, friends, neighbors, co-workers in an attempt to collect the debt.

If you feel you are being harassed by a creditor, report it promptly to the Federal Trade Commission (FTC), Better Business Bureau and state Attorney General.

More Money Saving Tips

Credit card companies make the bulk of their money off of the wannabees: people who want to live "The American Dream" but can't afford to buy it with cash. The interest you pay to borrow money from them is the profit they keep. Remember this every time you pull out that charge card to buy something. Use restraint and you'll come out ahead.

Avoid impulse spending. Leave credit cards at home unless making a specific purchase. Pay for everyday expenses with cash, check or debit card. Unless it's an emergency, only charge the things you can pay off in one or two months. If you can pay your full balances every month, choose a card which doesn't charge an annual fee.

More is not better! If you have difficulty resisting the urge to charge everything in sight, get rid of most of your credit cards. Cut them in half. Pay off your lowest balances first and close the accounts. Keep only one or two cards for emergencies.

Contact your state **Banking Department** to obtain a comparative listing of credit card rates, fees and grace periods. If you find a credit card company with lower rates than yours, consider transferring your balances.

If you are tired of receiving credit card offers, you have the right to exclude your name from the lists of names pre-screened by credit reporting agencies. You can choose to exclude your name from these lists for two years at a time, or permanently. To remove your name: **Automated Opt Out Request Line: (800) 353-0809**.

Take it to The Bank!

It may be a good time to comparison shop the banks for the lowest rates. Commercial banks tend to be more expensive and often require a high minimum balance to waive monthly fees. Community banks offer better rates, but may charge you more for things like ATM withdrawals and debit transactions. Read all mailings sent to you by your bank. These mailings may give notice of rate increases, new charges and changes to your account. Make sure you know exactly what you're paying to keep the account open. If you can find a bank which offers you more for your money, switch banks. Do this near the end of the month to avoid more fees.

See if you can join a credit union. Call the **Credit Union National Association** at: (800) 356-9655 to locate credit unions in your area. You may be able to save money on both your banking and credit card fees. Do your research because some credit unions don't offer a full range of services. Also, credit unions may not be as conveniently located as the larger banks.

www.creditinfocenter.com (Credit Info Center) Is a site where you can obtain information on bankruptcy, card/mortgage rates, consumer credit counseling services, credit cards, credit reports, loans and mortgage, rebuilding/repairing credit, scam alerts and more.

If you are having credit problems, you might find it beneficial to contact the **National Foundation for Consumer Credit.** (800) 388-2227 **www.nfcc.org** and find out what they can do for you.

You might also call **Consumer Credit Counseling Services**, a national, non-profit organization which provides free or low-cost counseling. (800) 388-CCCS.

Consumer Power: Mouth where your Money is.

Another element of successful money management is making sure you get the most for your dollar whenever you do spend. Ideally, you should get the best quality merchandise/service possible at the lowest possible price. You should also know what you are entitled to for your money, your rights as a consumer and what to do if you're being taken for a ride. This is what an educated consumer is all about.

As the consumer, you have the ultimate control and ultimate say when making a purchase. Never let anyone convince you otherwise. Some businesses will attempt to prey on you and approach you as if they're doing you a favor by taking your money. Some will go so far as to assume you're ignorant and will settle for anything. They use a range of tactics to intimidate and confuse you so you'll quickly make a purchase and go. Or, they want you to keep a purchase you've made even though you're not satisfied. In short, an *uneducated* consumer is their biggest customer and they want you to remain in the dark.

If you are spending money on something, regardless of its cost, you have the right to be satisfied. If you do not know or exercise your rights as a consumer, you've as good as given those rights away. It doesn't matter what your income is or how much you can afford to spend. You as an individual have the ultimate power to make or break a business. Realize and remember this and you will fully experience the feeling of power.

What many businesses don't want you to know is that they need you a whole lot more than you need them. No business can survive without customers, not even the largest company you can think of. When you make it clear to a vendor that you know your rights and you are ready to take your dollars elsewhere, you fully utilize your spending power. The business will respond and you will ultimately get what you want for your money.

It's the squeaky wheel that gets the grease!

In other words, the one refuses to stay quiet will get satisfaction. Persistence overcomes resistance. This is a very simple principle that works. Why not try it?

Tap the Power of The Pen!

It is truly amazing what one can accomplish by writing letters. You don't need great writing skills, all you need to do is organize your ideas, state the facts and ask for what you want. Many people have difficulty putting their thoughts on paper. If you're not the best letter-writer, ask someone you know for help. No shame in your game, just get the job done.

Writing a letter to a company can be effective because letters are legal documents that can be presented in court. Companies are well aware of this and will normally respond by calling or writing within a reasonable amount of time. When you write to a company, keep a copy of your letter and their written response, if any, until your issue is resolved.

Always go to the source. If you want quick results, bypass the employees and the manager and address the president or owner. Express your dissatisfaction with the product or services you received. Be as specific as possible about dates, names, etc. Let the owner know that you will neither purchase from them again (or use their services) nor will you recommend them to your friends and relatives. This will usually evoke a prompt response. If you feel you have been taken advantage of, state what you want and what your next course of action will be, such as contacting the state Attorney General and Federal Trade Commission. Believe me when I say you will not be ignored.

The same applies when you deal with a situation in person. You know you are entitled to satisfaction, keep your mind focused on that. Your best weapon is to stay calm, cordial and collected, no matter what. Some tacky businesses will try to anger you so you can lose your cool. Once you lose your cool, you've lost the game. Stay calm and in control. Think of all the agencies you plan to contact to report the business and smile.

Always begin by politely asking for the name of the person you're dealing with (salesperson, secretary, etc.). Get a full name, if possible.

A business should have its license(s) and certificate(s) to operate posted in plain view. In many states, it is a requirement by law. If the person does not give you their name or the name of the owner, you can usually obtain owner information from these documents.

Be nice, but be persistent. Remember, you can catch more flies with honey than with vinegar. Attempt to resolve the issue with the first person before taking it to the next level. Don't get frustrated if you do not achieve your goal at this point. Remember, you still have other options and will exhaust them all, if necessary.

If the store owner or company refuses to address your problem or give you owner information, calmly leave the establishment and return with a police officer. Get the officer's name, precinct and badge number and explain the problem. Ask to fill out a police report and don't be put off. The officer may be bound by law to file a report if you request it. If so, you'll have a credible witness in the event you decide to take your case to court.

If the business you are dealing with is a large-name franchisee (independently-owned), contact the parent company and complain. You can usually get the company's number and address from their product labels or toll-free information. If a company receives too many complaints about an independently-owned store, the store can lose its franchise. You'll probably receive a response and some compensation for your troubles.

Avoid buying from stores and businesses which insult you by offering you inferior quality goods and poor service. Avoid buying from stores and businesses which separate you from cheap merchandise with bullet-proof glass. Stores with bullet-proof glass assume you don't have the pride or the sense to shop elsewhere. Show them they're wrong. If you can, travel the extra distance to the store that appreciates your business and is willing to provide you with the proper service.

Just because a store posts a sign notifying you of a particular policy, doesn't mean the sign or policy are lawful. Many people mistakenly believe a sign posted in an establishment indicates a lawful policy. This is not necessarily so. A store's policy is not enforceable by law if the policy is in *itself* unlawful. If you have trouble with an establishment and are suspicious about its policies, don't hesitate to question them and take legal action. As a general rule, if a policy doesn't sound right to you, it probably isn't. Trust your judgment and get the facts.

The Fair Credit Billing Act (FCBA) is a law designed to protect consumers who pay for purchases with a credit card. Take full advantage of this law. Educate yourself as a consumer and demand satisfaction for your money.

Use a credit card to make large purchases and if you are unfamiliar with a company. If you have problems with the purchase, you can dispute the charges with the credit card company. If you do not have a credit card, ask someone else with a card to make a large purchase for you in exchange for cash. Your recourse in the event of a problem will remain the same, except the other person will have to dispute the charges on your behalf. More information on credit card disputes (chargebacks) follows later in this section.

Make sure you feel comfortable with a company before placing an order by phone, mail or over the internet. Review the merchant's policy on payments, charges and refunds. Make sure the product you want to purchase is available and you know the full total of the order.

There are laws which govern how mail-order, internet and phone sales merchants must conduct business such as **The Mail or Telephone Merchandise Order Rule**. This law covers merchandise you order by mail, phone, computer and fax. Once you place an order and give a merchant credit card information, the merchant is obligated by law to:

- Ship your order within the time stated in its ads or when promised to you at the time of the order.

- Ship the order within a specific amount of time after charging your credit card (possibly 48-72 hours).

- Notify you if the item you ordered is unavailable, give you an availability date/ship date and allow you to cancel the order if you do not wish to wait.

There are a number of other laws a credit card merchant must follow. As these laws vary from state to state, you will have to do some homework to find out the particulars in your state. In addition, you can contact the organizations listed in this chapter. I've used the services of these agencies and have found them to be very patient and helpful.

If you order merchandise from a company by mail, phone, internet or any other means for that matter, and you encounter problems with the merchandise after your credit card is charged, you have several options:

- Contact your credit card company and dispute the charge. The credit card company will be obligated to contact the vendor and attempt to resolve the issue within a certain amount of time. Under the law, you may withhold payment on the disputed item for as long as the charge is in dispute. This is often referred to as a "chargeback".

- Contact your state Attorney General. Write a letter explaining the situation and ask for an investigation.

- Contact the Federal Trade Commission (FTC) and file a complaint. (See next page for the FTC address.)

- Contact your local Better Business Bureau and file a complaint. (BBB web address appears on page 121.)

- Contact the agency which licenses the business and ask how you can file a complaint with the agency.

- Contact your local Consumer Protection Agency and the Consumer Protection Agency in the state where the merchant is located.

- Contact the Postal Inspector. Call or visit your local post office and ask for the Inspector-in-Charge.

- Consider trying to recoup your money through small claims court.

- You can also write The Direct Marketing Association (DMA) for help (see next page).

DMA Mail Order Action Line
1101 17th Street, NW, Washington, DC 20036

To lodge a formal online complaint against a company log onto: **www.ftc.gov** or, write/call:

FTC Consumer Response Center
600 Pennsylvania Avenue, NW
Washington, DC 20580
(877) FTC HELP/(877) 382-4357/(202) 326-2502/3650

www.bbb.org (The Better Business Bureau)
www.sec.gov/enforce/comctr.htm

In the event you are the victim of a scam, suspect a company of internet fraud or want to learn more:

www.consumerworld.org a public service site for tips, advice and other forms of help and information.

www.scambusters.com (Scambusters) Call: (800) 780-0090 Netrageous, Inc. (301) 570-5400.

www.scamwatch.com (Scam Watch) Log on for Web Police, Scamwatch, Web University, Women's World and more. General number: (317) 823-0377. Emergencies and Web Police: (317) 319-4038 (24 hrs).

www.internetfraudcouncil.org (Internet Fraud Council).

www.nationalfraud.com (National Fraud Center) (800) 999-5658/(215) 657-0800

Tired of Junk Mail? If you are tired of receiving tons of junk mail and picking up the phone just to hear an unsolicited sales pitch, read on. You can remove your name from national direct mail lists as well as your telephone number by writing a letter to:

DMA Mail Preference Service
P.O. Box 9008 Farmingdale, NY 11735-9008

The **Consumer Information Catalog** published by the U.S. Consumer Information Center lists free and low-cost booklets on many topics including home buying, education, travel, housing, children, cars, personal finance, investment and more. Ask for their free catalog: (888) 878-3256 or visit: **www.pueblo.gsa.gov** to view publications and place orders. You might also read:

The Consumer Bible, 1001 Ways to Shop Smart, by Mark Green, published by Workman Publishing.

Smart Money Decisions by Max H. Bazerman, published by Mark Wiley & Sons.

Investor Education Sites

www.aaii.com (American Association of Individual Investors) Free material. More with membership.

www.cbs.marketwatch.com (CBS Marketwatch) An online textbook teaches you basic to complex investing principles.

www.fool.com (The Motley Fool) Financial information and stock tips both the layman and avid financier can appreciate.

www.invest-faq.com (The Investment Faq) Type in a question or choose from a list of categories.

www.iown.com Check your credit, apply for prequalified mortgage, relocation services, compare mortgage rates, calculate closing costs.

www.investorwords.com (InvestorWords) You can look up inter-linked definitions to over 5,000 terms.

www.vanguard.com/educ/inveduc.html (Access Vanguard) This site offers a 10-course interactive program on investment fundamentals.

"A sure-fire way to double your money: fold it in half, stick it in your purse!"

Another Page in my Personal Chapter...

Suggestions: List three immediate financial goals and five long-term financial goals. What would be some realistic ways to achieve those goals? What are my obstacles and how can I work to overcome them?

_____

_____

_____

_____

_____

_____

_____

_____

_____

_____

_____

_____

_____

_____

_____

_____

This is YOUR personal page. Write on! ✎ *More space on the reverse...*

To Bear Fruit
Tips on Parenting for the Caring Mother

They say the apple doesn't fall far from the tree.
If the tree is mighty, so shall the fruit be.

Having a child can be the most blessed event in a woman's life. If she is truly ready to take that step, her life will change in the most amazing and wonderful ways. To give of oneself totally, to love and nurture another unconditionally is truly divine. As the child grows and develops into someone worthwhile, the mother receives one of life's most precious rewards.

Unfortunately, too many women have children for the wrong reasons, such as an attempt to hold onto a man, because of peer or family pressure, to feel needed, or just to have something to love. Some women are simply careless and refuse to practice safe sex. Others have children to receive public assistance and avoid keeping a real job. Unless they can ultimately devote themselves to motherhood, all these woman are doing themselves and their children a great disservice.

When a woman has a child for the wrong reasons, the child can become entangled in a web of confusion and not receive the nurturing it needs and deserves. The child is innocent, yet it carries the burden of blame. Some mothers become very resentful of the change in lifestyle real parenthood brings and their resentment manifests itself as neglect or abuse. If you're planning to have a child, look before you leap. Have you asked yourself...

What are my real reasons for wanting a child?

What kind of parent will I be?

Can I make a lifelong commitment to someone else?

Will I be able to fully uphold that commitment?

Am I ready to put someone else's needs before my own?

Am I prepared for a child financially?

What can I offer a child spiritually?

How will I nurture a child emotionally?

What are my values and how will I teach them?

If you haven't asked yourself these questions, you probably aren't ready to become a parent. Having a baby doesn't make you more of a woman, nor does it indicate any special talent. How you raise your child as a parent says more about you than the act of having a child itself. Being a dedicated parent may be the most difficult challenge you will ever face in your life. You must become selfless and offer your child unconditional love, every day that you live. Can you honestly do that?

Preparing for Motherhood

Once you've decided to have a baby and are pregnant, you want to make sure your baby has the best possible start in life. This is where good prenatal care comes in. Begin to monitor your pregnancy with your doctor as soon as possible. Make a commitment to take care of yourself physically. By receiving medical care early and taking the following precautions, you can help to ensure the health of both you and your precious baby.

- Eat a balanced diet rich in calcium, iron & vitamins.
- Don't smoke.
- Don't use illegal drugs.
- Don't drink alcohol.
- Don't take drugs not prescribed by your doctor.
- Practice safe sex, especially with someone you don't know well or fully trust. Mother and baby come first.

The **Planned Parenthood Federation of America** founded in 1916, offers a wide range of services for women including pregnancy tests, prenatal care, screening and treatment for sexually-transmitted diseases, counseling, birth control, termination of pregnancy and more. Call (800) 230-PLAN to get information about the Planned Parenthood affiliate in your area, log onto the website **www.plannedparenthood.org** or contact:

Planned Parenthood Federation of America
810 Seventh Avenue
New York, NY 10019
(212) 541-7800 • **www.ppfa.org/ppfa**

In addition to health center listings, the website contains information on job opportunities and the Legislative Action Center where you can express your views on reproductive health issues to Capitol Hill.

Teenagers exploring sexuality and relationship issues will enjoy logging onto: **www.teenwire.org**. Sponsored by Planned Parenthood, this award-winning website includes news, articles, Clinic Connections and more.

After Your Delivery...

After your delivery, see your OB/GYN or health care provider within 5-6 weeks and make an appointment for your baby to be seen by a pediatrician at two weeks of age. If you begin to feel overwhelmed by emotional stress, don't be afraid or ashamed to reach out for help. Speak to your doctor or social worker. Postpartum depression is an illness that can be treated.

As your child grows, do everything in your power to ensure his or her health and welfare. The **National Maternal and Child Health Clearinghouse** will provide free information and printed materials on maternal and child health. Call: (703) 821-8955. Also refer to the various listings beginning on page 130.

Preparing for Emergencies

According to The American Red Cross, injury is the leading cause of death of children in the United States.[1] Many infants and young children also die each year from poisoning and as a result of choking on a foreign object. Have a plan for dealing with emergencies. Keep the number for your local poison control center handy. One such number to call is: (800) 764-7661. It would also be wise to learn emergency care, including CPR, care for breathing difficulties and choking rescue for an infant aged birth to 1 year. Contact your local Red Cross chapter for information on first aid & safety courses or log onto: **www.redcross.org**. You can also contact their national headquarters at: 1621 North Kent Street, Arlington, VA 22209 (703) 248-4214.

The Consumer Product Safety Commission evaluates the safety of products sold to the public. They also provide printed materials on consumer product safety topics. To request these materials, call: (800) 638-CPSC.

Education is The Key to Success!

One of the greatest gifts you can give your child is the opportunity to receive a good education. Although private school is desirable, your child need not attend one in order to excel. Stay involved with the child's educational experience and your son or daughter will succeed. You have to be in for your child to win!

The Children's Scholarship Fund is a nationwide program designed to expand educational opportunities for families. The program works with partnerships and local groups in cities across the U.S. Children in grades Kindergarten through 8 can go to any private school

---

[1] American Red Cross Community First Aid and Safety Booklet, published by Mosby Lifeline. ISBN: 0-8016-7064-0.

that's eligible for scholarship funding. Scholarships are awarded based on financial need, applications selected by random drawing. The parent must gain the child's admittance to a school before seeking funding. For more information, call: 1-800 805-KIDS.

As the formative years are crucial, enroll a young child in day care, head start or a kindergarten program. Make reading a priority and read to and with your child. The **American Library Association** offers a number of free brochures and an annual listing of recommended reading entitled; "Notable Books for Children". Call the ALA directly at: (800) 545-2433 or (312) 944-6780. The ALA also has a website: **www.ala.org**. Also see the websites: **www.ucalgarv.ca/-dkbrown/index.html** and **www.soemadison.wisc.edu/ccbc/**.

From the moment your child is born, you should be planning and saving for your child's future, particularly, the child's college education. The earlier you begin to save and invest, the better. A good first step would be to learn a little about investing and then seek the help of an experienced financial advisor. You'll also find some useful information in the chapter, *Money Madness.*

There are many ways to save for you child's college education, from IRA's (Individual Retirement Accounts), to incentive plans offered by your state (State Savings Programs). Contact your state Department of Education to find out if a State Savings Program exists. Some states are listed below. Also see: **www.finaid.org.**

New York College Tuition Savings Program: (877) 697-2837
Better Educational Savings Trust (New Jersey): (877) 465-2378
Golden State Scholarship Trust (California): (877) 728-3433
Louisiana START: (800) 259-5626
Virginia Education Savings Trust: (888) 567-0540

The most important role model in your child's life will always be Y-O-U! Following is the list of parent re-sources mentioned earlier, many of these organizations offer free programs, assistance and referrals.

Extra-Curricular / Recreation

Big Brothers/Big Sisters of America (215) 567-7000 **www.bbbsa.org**

Boys & Girls Club of America (404) 815-5700 **www.bgca.org**

Boy Scouts of America (972) 580-2000 **www.bsa.scouting.org**

Camp Fire Boys and Girls (816) 756-1950 **www.campfire.org**

Girl scouts of the USA (212) 852-8000 **www.girlscouts.org**

National Association of Police Athletic Leagues (PAL) (561) 844-1823

Youth Achievement and Development

Association of Junior Leagues, Inc. (212) 683-1515

Center for Youth as Resources (202) 466-6272 **www.yar.org**

Girls Inc. (212) 509-2000 **www.girlsinc.org**

National Youth Leadership Council (612) 631-3672
www.mightymedia.com/edunet/nylc

YouthBuild USA (617) 623-9900 **www.youthbuild.org**

Education

Communities in Schools (703) 519-8999 **www.cisnet.org**

Educators for Social Responsibility (800) 370-2515

National PTA (312) 670-6782 **www.pta.org**

Youth/ Social Services

Bethesda Family Services Foundation **www.bsfs.org/bethesda**

Child Welfare League of America (202) 638-2952 **www.cwla.org**

Children's Defense Fund (202)628-8787 **www.childrensdefense.org**

National Network for Youth (202) 783-7949
www.nn4youth@.aol.com

Youth Service America (202) 296-2992 **www.servenet.org**

Drug Prevention

D.A.R.E. America (800) 223-DARE **www.dare-america.com**

Drug Policy Information Clearinghouse (800) 666-3332

National Parents Resource Institute for Drug Education
(800) 853-7867 **www.prideusa.org**

Violence and Crime Prevention

Fight Crime Invest in Kids (202) 638-0690 **www.fightcrime.org**

Gang Resistance Education and Training
www.atf.treas.gov/great.htm

Nat'l Center for Conflict Resolution Education (217) 384-4118

Street Law, Inc. (202) 293-0088 **www.streetlaw.org**

Youth Crime Watch of America (305) 670-2409 **www.ycwa.org**

Medical

American Academy of Pediatrics (847) 228-5005 **www.aap.org**

Centers for Disease Control and Prevention (404) 639-3311
www.cdc.gov

National Adolescent Health Resource Center (612) 627-4488

Other

National committee to Prevent Child Abuse (312) 663-3520

Barrios Unidos (408) 457-8208 **www.mercado.com**

Center for the Community Interest (202) 785-7844
www.communityinterest.org

Congress of National Black Churches, Inc. (202) 371-1091

National Center for Neighborhood Enterprise (202) 518-6500

National Civic League **www.ncl.org/ncl**

National Family Partnership (800) 282-7035

Parents Anonymous (The Nat'l Organization) (909) 621-6184
www.parentsanonymous-natl.org

 Being a parent is a lifelong commitment and can be very difficult, an endless struggle that never seems to get any easier. If you ever feel the pressures are becoming unbearable, take action immediately. Reach out and explore the many resources available to you. In the end, your family will benefit. You can survive and thrive!

If you have a missing child or lost child, contact Scam Watch at: **www.scamwatch.com** (International child center. MAD, Lost child, Youth Watch and a number of volunteer services). **Lost child emergency phone:** (317) 541-1542.

ᘓMothers... Log On!

Ask Jeeves for children is a web search engine for 7-14 year olds. Editorially selected questions and answers are combined with a screened metasearch. Ask Jeeves for Children was picked by PC Magazine as the best children's search engine of 1998. Log onto: **www.ajkids.com.**

www.zerotothree.org (National Center for Infants, Toddlers and families) Nonprofit site dedicated to child development from birth to age 3. Scheduled chats with baby experts.

www.parentsoup.com (iVillage) Tools for parenting. Also see their site: **www.parentsplace.com.**

Today's Joke Quote: "Learn from your parent's mistakes... use birth control!"

Health Wealth

Few people would argue that good health is a person's most valuable asset. This chapter and the ensuing *In Search of Healing* promote health and encourage you to improve your overall fitness. You have *Delilah Power!*, so use it!

Conscientious Dieting

"I didn't fight my way to the top of the food chain to become a vegetarian." (source unknown)

According to *Fitness Management* (April, 1999), obesity appears to be the result of a sedentary lifestyle rather than overeating. The reason: if you fail to exercise and burn calories, you store more fat. Many women believe skipping meals and going on radical diets will result in positive weight reduction. The truth is, any weight loss achieved by these means is probably temporary and potentially dangerous. What's more, not eating properly and lowering carbohydrate intake can actually cause you to *gain* weight. Starving your body of food, even for several hours, can create a condition known as *adipocyte hypertrophy*; your body slows its metabolism in response what it perceives as starvation and *increases* its fat storage.

Whenever you make a decision to go on a diet, you should know the various risks associated with weight loss. Any more than 1% of your total body weight lost in a week is excessive. If you want a permanent solution to a weight problem, you have to prepare yourself for a permanent, realistic lifestyle change and even behavior modification. Before beginning your diet, arrange for a routine check-up with your doctor.

A realistic diet involves learning to choose healthier (low fat/high fiber) foods from within normal food groups. This combined with a conscientious fitness program will increase your chances of long-term success. You must also avoid fatty foods. Fatty foods stimulate insulin production in the body, causing it to build up a pro-fat hormone which in turn, causes fat storage. As you work to improve your health and fitness, it would be wise to:

- Drink at least one large glass of water before meals. You'll become fuller on less food. Water will also aid in digestion, improve circulation and moisturize your skin, giving it a youthful glow.

- Eat vegetables first, meat second and starch last at every meal. Fill up on fiber and protein first.

- Consume several light meals rather than three heavy meals daily. This will help you to maintain constant energy levels and increase mental alertness.

- Avoid overdosing on vitamin supplements. Excessive amounts of Vitamin C for example, can cause the destruction of red blood cells, gout, impairment of white blood cells and more. The best way to get your essential vitamins and minerals: eat smart.

- Never go shopping for food when you're hungry.

Related Resource: The American Dietetic Association (800) 877-1600 **www.eatright.org**

Work that Body!

"Why work out? I get enough exercise just pushing my luck!"

Here's something to think about: studies have shown regular exercise and improved eating habits can actually *lower* your biological age. By staying fit throughout your lifetime, you'll lose less muscle mass and retain more strength as you grow older. You will also reduce your risk of a heart attack, diabetes, hypertension and other ailments.

Walking, dancing, bicycling, gardening, even cleaning the house can help you stay in great shape. You can also benefit by doing these simple exercises below.

Stretching the body before each workout helps to avoid injury. This exercise stretches the front of the thighs. Hold the position for ten seconds and switch legs. Keep chest lifted and pull foot gently. Breathe. Repeat.

Align the spine. Begin in this position and push buttocks forward. Exhale on the push. Keep your knees bent and chest listed. Hold for 3 seconds and return to original position. Try to feel when the spine is straight. Repeat the push ten times, switching your hand position each time.

Build thigh muscles, avoid knee injuries. Keep chest lifted, bend standing leg slowly. Hold for as long as possible, then switch. 20 repetitions each leg.

You can do this exercise while watching T.V. Find a comfortable position on your side. Raise the straight leg from floor slowly, hold 3 seconds and lower slowly. Switch sides. Do 10 repetitions on each leg, 3 times.

Slim the waistline. Hold position 5 seconds, lower head. Try doing ten repetitions and then switch sides. Repeat 3 times.

Open the pelvis and increase flexibility. Gently move into this position and hold for one minute. Deep breathing helps muscles relax. Perform daily.

Note: Exercising should never be excruciating. If you feel severe pain while exercising, stop and consult a physician. Avoid exercising if you are sick or injured.

Remember: drink lots of water to stay hydrated. Hydrate with sports drinks to avoid an electrolyte imbalance during heavy exercise.

Back in Action

Your spine supports your entire body and is subject to constant strain and stress. If your back is in pain, you can't function properly. Ways to watch your back:

- Maintain proper posture. Tip: Write *"P"* on your palm each morning for one week as a reminder.

- Lift objects carefully: bend knees and keep your waist straight to use your powerful thigh muscles.

- Strengthen your stomach. A strong stomach will act as a splint for a weak back.

- Engage in low-impact exercises.

- Don't stand or sit in one position for too long. Move around, get up and stretch at least once every hour.

- Sit in firm chairs that support the back, put a rolled towel or pillow between your low back and the chair.

- Shed those extra pounds if you are overweight. Excessive weight can really aggravate the spine.

- Avoid very flat shoes and stiletto pumps. Make sure your sneakers offer support and fit properly. Wear soft-soled shoes with low heels.

- Follow these sleeping tips: when lying on your back, put a pillow under your knees. If lying on your stomach, place a pillow beneath your hips. If you sleep on your side, keep legs bent and place a pillow between your thighs or knees. After only one night of sleeping this way, you will notice a big difference in the way your back feels.

Your Back: An Owners Manual is a free publication available from the Baylor College of Medicine. Send a stamped, self-addressed envelope to the Office of Promotion, 1 Baylor Plaza, Room 176B, Houston Texas 77030 or call: (713) 798-5770.

Always check with your doctor before beginning any new fitness regimen. Exercise moderately and don't overdo it. Choose activities that are convenient and fun and make them a part of your regular routine. Remember, fitness is a lifelong goal!

BREAST SELF-EXAMINATION
A Guide for Today's Woman

STEP 1:
Visual
Examination

In front of a mirror, arms at your side, look at both breasts carefully for puckering, dimpling, scaling, skin color change or fluid around the nipple.

Clasping hands behind your head, press forward, tightening the chest muscles. Repeat a careful visual inspection.

Press hands firmly down on hips, again tightening chest muscles. Repeat a careful visual inspection. *Remember, it is normal for one breast to look slightly different from the other. Monthly practice will teach you what is normal for you.*

STEP 2:
"Clock Examination"
(Standing)

Most women prefer to do Step 2 in the shower. Raise your left hand and use three or four fingers of the right hand to examine the left breast. Beginning at the top outside edge, press with the flat part of your fingertips in a circular motion. Use firm, careful, thorough movements. Check for any lump, hard

knot or thickening. Move your fingers clockwise to a new position that overlaps slightly the area just examined. Repeat the process, moving in a clockwise fashion. Each circle will become progressively smaller as you move toward the nipple. An adequate examination requires *at least* four concentric circles or more—what-

ever is needed—to cover the breast. Finally, it is *very important* to explore the side of your breast where it extends up into the armpit. Use the same small, circular motion. Repeat the examination with your left hand and right breast. *Note: It is normal to feel a ridge of firm tissue around the lower curve of each breast.*

STEP 3:
"Clock Examination"
(Lying Down)

Lie on your back with your left arm over your head and a pillow or towel under the left shoulder. This position helps flatten and evenly

distribute the tissue. Use the right hand to repeat the clock examination of the left breast described above. Switch sides and repeat.

STEP 4:
Examine
the Nipple
(Standing)

By gently squeezing the nipple, you can see if any fluid is discharged from either side. If you notice a discharge, discuss this or any other finding with your physician.

REMEMBER: Do not hesitate to discuss anything that seems unusual with your doctor. You won't be a "bother," and what you report could be very important to your health.

Reprinted with the permission of the author.

More women are being diagnosed with breast cancer than ever before. Early detection saves lives. Examine your breasts regularly to help yourself stay healthy.

Pregnancy and Contraception

Were you aware that...

- Emergency contraception (which is also referred to as the "morning after pill") can be taken up to 72 hours after unprotected intercourse or a contraception failure such as a busted condom?
- The "morning after pill" is NOT the same as the European abortion pill (RU-486)?
- Regular birth control pills can be taken in a specific quantity to provide emergency contraception? (You must get a prescription and instructions from a doctor.)
- Your window of fertility is about six days: the *five days before* ovulation *and* the day of ovulation? (Your most fertile time of month is the middle of your menstral cycle.)

If you have reason to believe you're pregnant, see a doctor or visit your area health clinic immediately. Do not attempt to use emergency contraception to terminate a pregnancy or replace the responsible use of regular birth control. If you'd like to learn more about emergency contraception and the European abortion pill (RU-486), log onto: **www.onhealth.com** (OnHealth). Also investigate:

The Center for Reproductive Law and Policy: **www.crlp.org**. Their headquarters: 120 Wall St. NYC (212) 514-5534.

The American Society for Reproductive Medicine: (800) 255-6014, **www.asrm.org**.

The American Medical Women's Association: **www.amwa-doc.org**. Headquarters: (800) 995-2692.

The right to reproductive freedom is yours. For more regarding pregnancy, prenatal care and children, review the chapter, *To Bear Fruit*.

Know Your Body

As long as you're sexually active, you run the risk of sexually transmitted diseases, pregnancy and AIDS. Even if you're in a serious relationship or marriage, you cannot guarantee the fidelity of your partner. The best way to stay safe: use a condom.

Always check your vaginal discharges and odor so that you are very familiar with both. If you notice any changes in either, or experience itching, burning or redness in the vaginal area, contact your doctor or visit your local health clinic.

Here's a brief list of ailments and sexually transmitted diseases you can contract by failing to protect yourself:

AIDS: Acquired Immune Deficiency Syndrome. Currently incurable.

Chlamydia: can cause Pelvic Inflammatory Disease (PID), stillbirths and male sterility. Symptoms resemble those of gonorrhea.

Crabs (pubic lice): easy to catch and spread, not as dangerous as other STD's, but very annoying. Can still spread with condoms.

Genital Herpes: strain(s) of the varicella virus. Not life threatening, but can increase your risk of AIDS and other STD's. If active, can harm your baby during delivery. Incurable.

Genital Warts: caused by papillomavirus. Left untreated, can cause Cervical Dysplasia (abnormal growths on the cervix) and cancer.

Gonorrhea: many women have no symptoms, but can spread it. Can lead to serious health problems if left untreated.

Hepatitis B: more dangerous and easily contracted than AIDS.

HIV: the virus which is believed to cause AIDS.

Scabies: nasty parasites which can make life miserable.

Syphilis: progresses through 3 stages. Its symptoms often go undetected. Untreated to the 3rd stage, can cause death.

Trichomoniasis: more serious than a yeast infection. If left untreated, can lead to Pelvic Inflammatory Disease (PID) and infertility.

Yeast infections: the result of an overgrowth of micro-organisms in the vagina. Caused by stress, hormonal changes, pregnancy, weak immune system (HIV, AIDS and diabetes), increased sexual activity and taking antibiotics. Itchy and annoying, but treatable.

Prescription Drugs and Over the Counter Medication

Here are some important things to know about prescription and non-prescription drugs:

- Certain foods can reduce the effectiveness of some medications. Conversely, some medicines lower your body's absorption of specific nutrients.
- Non-steroidal, anti-inflammatory drugs (such as aspirin) can cause deadly ulcers/stomach problems.
- Certain herbs/herbal remedies can interfere with the effectiveness of medications.
- The generic version of a drug may not be exactly the same as the brand-name. Always ask your doctor to prescribe the brand-name drug and write "DAW" or, *Dispense As Written* on all your prescriptions. If you accept a generic drug, ask your pharmacist if the drug is "bioavailable" (comparable in its rate of absorption/interaction with other drugs) and "bioequivalent" (comparable in its physiological effects with the brand name counterpart).

It's Time to See a Doctor when You Have:

- difficulty breathing and/or chest pressure combined with sweating
- sudden changes in vision
- physical clumsiness or mental confusion
- blood in urine or stool
- significant changes in weight or body shape
- persistent cough or fever
- unexplained and/or persistent pain
- piercing headache
- feelings of fatigue or sadness not helped by sleep or change of events.
- any other reason to think you may be ill.

Another Page in my Personal Chapter...

Health is unquestionable wealth. Your body is your temple, so take some time to worship it! Suggestions: Map out plans for an improved physical fitness program right now. What part(s) of the body will receive your immediate attention?

_____

_____

_____

_____

_____

_____

_____

_____

_____

_____

_____

_____

_____

_____

_____

This is YOUR personal page. Write on! ✎ *More space on the reverse...*

In Search of Healing

There comes a time in every woman's life when she has to seek medical intervention for an illness. Because you have *Delilah Power!* you can take your own health initiatives and make wiser decisions regarding your care.

According to a number of studies, Black people in the U.S. die disproportionally from preventable or treatable illnesses. We're also at higher risk for AIDS, diabetes and other ailments. Even after diagnosis, we often receive inferior, or less aggressive care than whites. When you need medical treatment, the key to receiving quality care is *assertiveness*. It's *your* body and *your* health. It's therefore *your* right to:

- Know the details of your illness.
- Know what treatment options are available including "alternative treatments" (homeopathic, visualization and meditation, hypnotherapy and psychic healing).
- Review the credentials of your doctor and all others involved in your care.
- Consult with other doctors and professionals.
- Get a second opinion when surgery is recommended.
- Change doctors or hospitals at any time.
- Make your own decisions regarding your care and treatment.

While having faith in your doctor is important, you should still have an intense curiosity about your body. Many doctors operate under the assumption you don't want or need to know everything. Some will even treat your body like a mystery only *they* have the power to unlock. Unless you request certain information from a physician, you won't necessarily get it.

If you have an illness that will require surgery or a hospital stay, try to shop for a doctor and hospital. Some questions you might ask a doctor are:

- What is your experience in treating my particular illness or condition?
- Do you recommend treatments and therapies that don't rely heavily on medication?
- What are the decision-making procedures? Will you be comfortable with my involvement in the decision-making process?
- What are your ethical, religious and philosophical views?
- Are you familiar, comfortable and sensitive to my cultural background?

The hospital you choose should have proven expertise. The more they perform similar procedures to yours, the better. Many hospitals have their own websites and the information you find there can help you to determine the institution's competence. Also log on to:

www.healthfinder.gov (U.S. Department of Health and Human Services) Help and information including a medical dictionary and links to the National Institutes of Health.

Another way to check out hospitals would be to call a nearby medical school, speak to the chairman of the relevant department and ask for a referral. You can also read printed guides on hospitals. Some people feel the best referrals are those by word of mouth.

Once you've chosen a hospital, contact a physician who is on the hospital's board of directors and ask for a consultation. You should also see (or have a family member talk to) the hospital administrator and a social worker. Ask if there's a *Patient's Bill of Rights* and if you can review it. If you are polite and appreciative, most hospital personnel will be very helpful.

Once you're admitted, be pleasant and communicative with the nursing staff. Since mistakes can be made, tell the head nurse you want to be informed *beforehand* of all medication or treatment being given to you. Review your bedside chart. When nurses administer medicine, check to ensure medication and dosages are accurate.

Preparing for Surgery

If you've been told you need surgery, ALWAYS get a second opinion. You should also interview, evaluate and investigate the prospective surgeon as follows:

- Has the doctor completed a residency that has been approved by the American Board of Surgery?

- Has the physician received board certification in his specialty from The American Board of Medical Specialties (ABMS), or a board under the aegis of the American Osteopathic Association (AOA)?

- Does the doctor have fellowship status in a college or university? A good sign of professional qualification.

- Is the doctor an attendee of a hospital and have admitting privileges? In many states, physicians can practice legally without any malpractice insurance. However, few hospitals permit doctors to become attendees unless they carry malpractice insurance.

After you've chosen a surgeon you're comfortable with, get as many details about the surgery as possible:

- What are the risks of this operation?
- What is the mortality rate for this operation?

- What are possible complications?
- Are there alternative treatments for my condition?
- How long will it take me to recover?
- How many of these operations have you done in your career? How many in the past year?
- Can you connect me with other people who've had the same operation so I can ask them questions? Do you know of any support groups?

Don't be intimidated. If the stress of your impending surgery is overwhelming, have someone accompany you to your appointments to listen in, take notes and give feedback. Utilize the support of family and friends.

Health Maintenance Organizations

Although some HMO's are rated higher than others, you can receive quality care from *any* doctor or clinic if you find out:

- What are the qualifications of the doctors?
- On average, what is the wait for an appointment?
- Is the center I'll be assigned to open on evenings and weekends? Where do I go in an emergency?
- Are lab work and X-rays performed in-office? What are the qualifications of the people doing the tests?
- What is the procedure to change doctors or centers?
- Does the doctor(s) accept patient phone calls?
- Is care provided for patients in the home?
- Is the office handicap accessible?
- Does the HMO cover me for emergency care while I'm traveling?
- Is there a deductible/co-payment required per visit?

As with hospitals, a visit to the center administrator's office can be very productive. Also contact the HMO's membership department with questions or concerns.

Preventive Medicine

Mounting evidence suggests many illnesses can be prevented through lifestyle changes. Your first defense against illness is prevention.

- Get a pelvic exam and pap smear every year.
- Examine your breasts monthly.
- Get tested for sexually transmitted diseases.
- Get mammograms yearly after age 40.
- Check your serum cholesterol.
- Get tested for diabetes, especially if there's a family history.
- Take regular tuberculosis tests.
- Keep your vaccinations up to date and get the yearly flu shot.
- Never put off seeing a doctor if you suspect something may be wrong with you.
- Follow normal health advice: quit smoking, don't use drugs, eat a balanced diet and exercise regularly.

Related Resources and Websites of Information

Our Bodies, Ourselves for the New Century, A book by and for women by The Boston Women's Health Book Collective, published by Simon and Schuster, Inc. ISBN: 0-6848423-1-9.

The PDR Family Guide to Women's Health and Prescription Drugs by Medical Economics. ISBN: 1-56363-086-9.

Every Woman's Guide to Prescription and Non Prescription Drugs, Guild America Books. ISBN: 1-56865-248-8.

www.accenthealth.com (AccentHealth) Site includes informative Healthwise Knowledgebase. Worth a go-see.

www.cdc.gov Centers for Disease Control and Prevention Find out more about AIDS in the Black community and other illnesses including sexually transmitted diseases.

www.diabetes.org/africanamerican Website of American Diabetes Association, African-American Program.

www.geocities.com/hotsprings/7880 (Friends for Friends, Inc.) A nonprofit organization dedicated to reducing the risk of HIV infection among African-Americans.

www.lungusa.org (The American Lung Association) Information about asthma and other ailments.

www.mayohealth.org supported by the Mayo Clinic.

www.onhealth.com (OnHealth) look up hundreds of articles and daily briefings on health issues.

www.niaid.nih.gov (the National Institute of Allergy and Infectious Diseases). Research and information.

Conquering Inner Beasts:

We all have beasts to conquer, both within and without. Many of these beasts stay our entire lifetimes, but that doesn't mean they can't be kept at bay. Inner strength, divine guidance and support from others can help us to triumph. It is up to each woman however, to know herself and acknowledge when help is needed.

There's a lot of pressure on a modern woman to be a number of things to a number of people: wife, mother, housekeeper, career professional and more. Sometimes, it's impossible to do it all. As a result, women can suffer from stress, depression, anxiety and other ailments, including what's called a Superwoman Complex.

Some stress is normal in everyday life, but too much stress is unhealthy. You know you're under too much stress when you:

- 💣 Can't sleep as a result of the stress.
- 💣 Can't eat.
- 💣 Can't focus on everyday tasks.
- 💣 Feel pent up, on the edge and/or about to explode.
- 💣 Feel unwell or show physical signs of stress such as losing your hair, breaking out in pimples, gaining or losing weight, etc.
- 💣 Feel otherwise unable to perform at optimum level.

There are many ways to combat stress, you must find those best suited for you. Remember: you can't take care of others until and unless you take care of *yourself.*

- 💣 Find a way to vent. Talk to a good friend about your problems and/or stress factors, write in a journal, get more exercise, have more sex.
- 💣 Avoid multi-tasking. Try to handle one job at a time and work at a reasonable pace.
- 💣 Focus on slowing down. Relaxing helps to reduce stress and lowers the risk of health problems, including high blood pressure.
- 💣 Acknowledge when you need help. It can be a sign of strength, not weakness to say; "I can't deal with this by myself."

Depression and Anxiety

It's normal to feel down or anxious at some time or other, but it isn't normal or healthy to suffer from long bouts of depression or anxiety. Depression and anxiety are caused by internal conditions which are treatable. Early diagnosis/intervention can help you to feel better.

If you suspect you may be suffering from depression or anxiety, see your doctor or contact the Mental Health

Crisis Hotline at: (800) 543-3638 or (212) 561-7000. For anxiety, you can get in touch with the office for Phobias, Obsessions and Mood Disorders at: (202) 787-6775.

Whenever you feel nervousness taking control, you can alleviate anxiety with this simple yet effective, controlled-breathing exercise:

Stand or sit still. Close your eyes. Focus on your breathing and your heartbeat. Inhale slowly and deeply, filling your entire chest cavity with air. Hold the air and count to three. Exhale slowly, concentrating on slowing the beat of your heart. Do this ten times, relaxing the body with each exhale.

Drug Abuse

If you have substance abuse problems, the time is NOW to conquer them. Attempting to escape your life with drugs and alcohol is an illusory solution. These beasts are incredibly powerful and will constantly feed on your dependency. As you become weaker, they grow even stronger: destroying mind, body and soul. Your life is far too precious to ruin. You *can* find meaning in your life and obtain happiness if you just reach out. Contact the organizations listed below.

Community Anti-Drug Coalitions of America: (800) 54-CADCA

D.A.R.E America: (800) 223-DARE

www.theantidrug.com: Office of National Drug Control Policy. Parenting brochure available.

National Clearinghouse on Alcohol and Drug Information: (301) 468-2600

The Partnership for a Drug Free America: **www.drugfree.america.org**.

Quote of the day: "Out of my mind... back in 5 minutes."

Working over Time

There is no better feeling than to earn your own money. Despite whatever negative feelings you may have about your job, working is healthy. A job can give you a firm sense of purpose and responsibility, foster independence and instill pride. Any situation is what you make it. A job can keep you busy and stimulate you. Most people need to stay busy in order to have a healthy mental attitude. We all complain about our jobs and probably wish we could be elsewhere. But the real truth is, we're a lot better off when we're presented with challenges and can find the motivation to overcome them.

If you are out of work and looking for a job, it can be a tiring and frustrating experience. You may be disgusted with yourself and others, angry at the world and pretty pessimistic about the future. Being broke is no fun at all and can lead to serious depression.

If you do not have the skills to do the job you would like, there may be ways to study a particular field and learn what you need to know. There are two types of unemployed people: those who claim they want a job, but never take the steps necessary to find one and those who spend time and energy investigating possible resources. When an opportunity presents itself, the second type of person seizes it and ends up with a skill, a job and self-respect. Which type of person are you?

Following are some resources you might utilize for finding a job or developing a skill.

Are you between the ages of 16-24? Did you drop out of high school or recently receive your high school diploma? Are you looking for a job? If so, **Job Corps** may be for you. Funded by the U.S. Department of labor, Job Corps has 10 regional offices in the country and local offices nationwide including Alaska, Hawaii and Puerto Rico. They can help you get your GED and offer over a hundred free vocational programs including

Health Occupations, Visual Arts, Data Entry, Clerical, Computer Technology, Carpentry, Masonry, and Food Service. In addition, you can benefit from basic education and social skills development. Below is a listing for the national office and a general toll-free number you can call for more details.

Job Corps / ETA Department of Labor
200 Constitution Avenue, NW, Washington, DC 20210
(800) 733-5627 – **www.jobcorps.org**

I learned how to type properly and use a computer by attending a free training program given by the State University of New York. Learning these skills influenced my decision to become a writer. I was out of work, strapped for cash and feeling lousy about myself when I decided it was time for change. I realized I needed to learn a marketable skill and fast. A part of me was afraid, but another stronger part insisted I take action. I read local newspapers, scanned television programs and asked around until I found the training program. The skills I acquired there were invaluable. Learning about computers helped me regain my self-confidence and I've used my acquired skills to write this book.

If you would like to learn a skill, contact your state's Department of Education or your state university and ask them if they have an **Equal Opportunity Center** in your city or any other training programs sponsored by the state. You may be surprised by what you find. If you live in the New York area, contact the State University of New York office in Manhattan:

State University of New York
Educational Opportunity Center in Manhattan
163 West 125th Street, New York, NY 10027
(212) 961-4400/4321

Another option: Give your state **Department of Labor** a call and ask them what brochures and programs are available. The Department of Labor can give you up-to-date info on job openings as well as training/apprentice opportunities, for free. Job placement services, job search guides, workshops and seminars which can include resume preparation, interviewing, marketing techniques and more are also available. Obtain full information on state, federal, county and city Civil Service examinations. You can often get the applications for Civil Service exams at any of the local Department of Labor offices.

Also ask your Department of Labor where the **Federal Employment Information Center** is in your area. At this center, you will be able to obtain more information about federal employment opportunities.

The Federal Career Directory provides information on federal careers and employment opportunities. You may find this booklet at the local library or purchase it by writing:

Superintendent of Documents
U.S. Government Printing Office
Washington, DC 20402 (202) 512-1800
Stock No. 006-000-01339-2

The Office of Personnel Management (OPM) has what's called **The Career America Connection** which provides information regarding federal job opportunities for people with college credits or a degree. Job categories include: Science, Special Services, Law Enforcement, Administration, Accounting. Career America Connection is available around the clock. (912) 757-3000.

If you have a personal computer and a modem, see what the **Federal Job Opportunities Bulletin Board** can do for you. Scan information online or download to your computer. Call: (912) 757-3100.

There is no shame in being unemployed unless you're capable of working, but have no intention of ever doing so. If you have children, you can inspire independence in them and encourage them to become enterprising, ambitious adults by keeping a regular job. This is the only way a family can truly prosper, each generation achieving more than the last. Make a worthwhile, lasting impression on your children. Believe in yourself and never give up. A skill and a great job are out there waiting for you. Remember, positivity breeds success!

www.jobsearch.org (The U.S. Department of Labor) called America's Job Bank, allows you to post one listing free of charge. The Career resources include: Career and Resource Library, Occupational Trends, Relocation Information & more.

Successful Interviewing

Once you have a skill and a job lined up, you face the challenge of passing the interview. There are a number of things you can to increase you chances of being hired. I spoke with a friend who works as a recruiter for an employment agency and she offered these tips for making a positive impression on a hiring executive:

Getting Ready

☞ Prepare a one-page resumé. The sole purpose of a resume is to summarize your education, training, skills and experience. Don't get fancy with it. You'll have time to give details about your qualifications during the interview.

☞ Convince yourself you are the person for the job and realize the company has much to gain by hiring you. The talents and skills you have to offer will make them more productive. Thinking this way will help you to feel more confident.

☞ Find out as much as you can about the company before the interview. Write out any questions you may have and memorize them for the face-to-face.

☞ Avoid wearing loud colors and prints. Play it safe by dressing conservatively in basic colors. Blue is a good choice as it is perceived as a color of power and authority. What you wear needn't be expensive, just clean and pressed. In addition, don't overdose on the perfume. Choose a scent that is light and airy.

☞ Aim to arrive 15 minutes early. This will allow you adequate time to get settled, compose yourself and survey the situation.

☞ Interview late in the afternoon, if possible. After seeing so many people in a day, the interviewer will be more inclined to remember you.

☞ Eat a light meal prior to the interview so that you feel and appear energetic.

Face to Face

☞ Upon entering the interviewer's office, smile, shake hands, address him or her by name and do not sit until he or she tells you to.

☞ Once seated, sit up attentively and learn forward.

☞ Do not chew gum.

☞ If you cross your legs, do so neatly with heels on the floor, under your chair, or toward the interviewer.

☞ Although you may feel nervous, try not to fidget.

☞ Make eye contact with the interviewer and maintain it while speaking. Your facial and eye expressions should remain friendly and responsive.

☞ Keep your hands where the hiring executive can see them. In non-verbal communication, this suggests you have nothing to hide and makes you appear trustworthy.

☞ Listen to the interviewer's questions carefully and respond thoughtfully. Nod your head as the interviewer speaks to show you're listening.

☞ Do not interrupt the interviewer.

☞ When prompted, ask questions you've prepared or any others you may have to demonstrate that you know something about the company and take the position you're interviewing for seriously.

☞ While salary may not be the very first issue you discuss, it's certainly one of the most important. If you're not clear on the salary, do not hesitate to inquire later in the interview.

☞ Thank the interviewer for his or her time and shake hands again upon leaving. Maintain eye contact.

☞ Follow up by calling the interviewer to thank him or her for the appointment. If possible, add something that wasn't discussed during the interview in order to reopen communication channels.

☞ A few days later, mail a brief thank you note to the interviewer.

When All's Said and Done...

Each interview you go on will be part of a valuable learning experience. Don't get discouraged if you're not chosen immediately for a job. Know that there will always be other opportunities. Persistence overcomes resistance! As you continue to search for work, you'll feel more comfortable with the interviewing process. When the right job for you comes along, it'll be yours!

Let ambition be your guide!

Hard work and determination always pays off. If you reach for the sky, you'll find yourself amongst the stars.

If you're uncertain of what type of job is ideal for you, you can get a better idea by taking a vocational interest test such as the *Strong-Campbell Interest Inventory* and the *Kudor Occupational Interest Inventory*. The results can help you decide which jobs will most likely satisfy you and predict your likelihood of staying in the field.

High schools and colleges will usually offer vocational interest tests free to their students and alumni through their guidance or career planning offices. You may also locate these interest tests at job and education centers. The assistance of a trained counselor might be needed to interpret the results.

Do your own personal investigating. Visit your library and read about different career options. Try talking to people who are already in the fields which interest you. The *Occupational Outlook Handbook*, published by the U.S. Department of Labor is an excellent reference for information and is often available at the library. Below are the fastest growing jobs in the U.S.

Fastest Growing Jobs, 1996-2006

Database Administrators/computer-support

Computer engineers

System Analysts/computer programmers

Personal and home care aids

Physical and corrective therapy assistants

Home health aids

Medical assistants

Desktop publishing specialists and web designers

Physical therapists

Occupational-therapy assistants and aids

Today's Quote: "I'm out of bed and dressed, what more do you want?"

Miscellaneous Web Sites of Interest

www.about.com (About.com)   News, info and entertainment site. Chat, discussions, forums, newsletters and event calendars.

www.amnh.org (American Museum of Natural History) This highly-rated, virtual science museum offers educational activities, Quick Time video clips and more.

www.anywho.com (Anywho) Directories by At&T Labs. Find current telephone numbers.

www.blackboard.com Free online course service. Create a virtual class, no programming or html knowledge necessary. Also browse the course catalog for courses anyone can take.

www.dejanews.com (Deja.com) "Share what you know and learn what you don't". Usenet communities. www.deja.com

www.edupoint.com (Edupoint.com) Education resource for working professionals.

www.encarta.msn.com (Encarta) Explore this web address for basic encyclopedia research.

www.exploratorium.edu (The Exploratorium) Visit online exhibits, watch videos, peruse digital library.

www.funny.com Log onto this site for a large collection of jokes. A good diversion after hours of work on the computer.

www.mos.org (Boston's Museum of Science) Online exhibits.

www.nvf.org (National Veterans Foundation) Resources and support for veterans and their families.

www.onelook.com (One Look) An online dictionary with over 2477983 words in 545 dictionaries indexed and growing.

www.switchboard.com (Switchboard) Here you can locate phone numbers, email addresses, neighborhood attractions and more.

www.tucows.com Download free software, shareware and freeware.

www.yourday.com Help yourself get organized.

Strawberry Soup Aphrodite™

Strawberry Soup Aphrodite is a fruity, chilled dessert, the preferred choice of the gods. For a heavenly taste experience, serve it to your Black Adonis. Hot nights and searing passion will prevail. To generate even more excitement, accompany with shortbread cookies or delicate chocolate wafers.

3 pints hulled, fresh strawberries
½ cup red wine or fruit liqueur (use your creative judgment)
½ cup sugar with wine, ¼ cup with liqueur
1 teaspoon minced fresh ginger or ½ teaspoon powdered
½ cup heavy cream (use 1 cup if you'd like it really creamy)
1 tablespoon chopped, fresh mint
1-2 tablespoons raspberry vinegar or white wine vinegar
Sliced fresh strawberries for garnish

In a 1-quart saucepan, bring wine, sugar and ginger to a boil. Lower heat and simmer for 5 minutes. Add heavy cream and return to boiling. Cook for 1 minute, stirring constantly. Remove the pan from heat. In a food processor or blender, mix strawberries, mint and vinegar until strawberries are pureed. Add cream mixture from other pot and blend until well mixed. Pour into an airtight container and leave in refrigerator until fully chilled.

This soup can last in the refrigerator for several days. To serve, place in glass bowls which have been chilled in the freezer for an hour or more. Serve immediately. Garnish with a strawberry slice or a spring of mint. Serves 4. Rating: ☆☆☆

Coochie Carrot Cake™

Keep him coming back with Coochie Carrot Cake. It's moist, juicy and sweet, just the way he likes it. Give him a taste and make him beg for a piece. If he doesn't lick the plate, make it your last date.

2 cups carrots, grated fine or shredded (about 6 large carrots)
½ cup chopped walnuts
½ cup raisins
½ cup butter, softened
1 cup dark brown sugar, firmly packed
2 large eggs
½ teaspoon cloves
½ teaspoon nutmeg
1 teaspoon cinnamon
1 teaspoon baking powder
½ teaspoon salt
1 cup flour

Mix walnuts, raisins and carrots in a large bowl. In another bowl, combine butter, sugar, eggs, cloves, nutmeg, cinnamon, baking powder and salt and beat until creamy. Add flour and mix until just blended. Add to carrot mixture and blend well. Place in greased, 9x9x2 inch baking pan or bundt pan. Bake 35 minutes at 350 degrees. Cool completely. Serves 12.

Cream Cheese Frosting:

1 package of cream cheese (3 oz), room temperature.
1 tablespoon milk
½ teaspoon vanilla or lemon extract
2 cups confectioners sugar

Beat all ingredients vigorously until smooth and creamy. Frost cooled cake. Makes 1½ cups frosting. Rating: ☆☆☆☆

College Bound

Going to college is a big step in a person's life and a dream for many. Unfortunately, some people visualize themselves attending college or receiving a degree, but think they could never afford it, or are afraid they don't qualify academically. The truth is, billions of dollars in grants, scholarships and loans are awarded to students every year. If you are serious about wanting to attend college, there is a way. This section may provide you with information that can help you. The rest depends solely upon you. In the end, persistence, determination and a positive attitude will help to get you enrolled in the school of your choice.

The Federal Student Information Center is a good place to begin. Contact them and ask for the free "College is Possible" Brochure (800) 433-3243 or log onto the **U.S. Department of Education's** website at: **www.collegeispossible.org**.

If you have an idea of what you want to study, you should begin investigating colleges which offer excellent instruction in that field. Many colleges are known for specific programs. If you are uncertain of what field you want to enter, you can choose a college with a good liberal arts program and explore several areas before making a final decision.

Your biggest concern will undoubtedly be the money involved. You will be faced with tuition, various fees and expenses throughout your academic career. If you attend a school out of state, you must also consider living expenses. There are a number of funding sources you can utilize to pay for college such as grants, work-study programs, loans and scholarships. Many students rely on a combination of these sources in order to complete their requirements and graduate. Once you have applied to a school, the financial aid office should be able to help you apply for financial assistance.

You would find it very wise to investigate potential sources of financial aid as soon as possible, even before you actually enroll in a college. With a bit of research, you may uncover valuable resources. Since loans have to be repaid, you want to apply for them as a last resort. What you really want are grants and scholarships. These do not have to be repaid, but will be given to you with a stipulation such as your maintaining a certain grade point average, or making a firm commitment to complete a degree program. The competition for free money is stiff, so apply for as many scholarships and grants as you possibly can.

For more information on financial aid for college, log onto: **www.nasfaa.org** National Association of Student Financial Aid Administrators.

USA Group supports access to education by providing financial, information and management services. They are the nation's largest student loan guarantor and administrator. Get financial aid tips and learn more about "America's Tuition Plan" at: **www.usagroup.com** or call: (800) 348-4607. Ask them to send you their free *Education Loan Guide* (800) 562-6872.

Another viable source is the **United Student Aid Fund** (800) 428-9250. Call and ask about the "Families Federal Loan Program".

You've probably heard of **The United Negro College Fund** (UNCF), but do you know what this organization can do for you? The UNCF is an African-American higher education assistance organization which awards scholarships to students attending its member colleges and universities. Students can apply for geographically-based scholarships, scholarships based on their academic major and scholarships based on merit and need. Many historically Black colleges in the U.S. are UNCF member schools. For more information contact: **UNCF** 8260 Willow Oaks Corporate Drive, Fairfax, VA 22031 (800) 642-2041 / (888) 716-4954 **www.uncf.org**.

Today's Joke Quote: "Hard work has a future payoff, laziness pays off NOW!"

162   *Practica*

If you feel a traditional college environment is not the option for you right now, why not investigate whether your state has an **Educational Opportunity Program** (EOP) by calling your State Education Department? You may be able to receive valuable job training skills. Students who are ineligible for admission to the state university under traditional standards are considered for EOP's. To qualify for these types of programs, you should show a strong desire and potential to complete college level work and have financial need. Usually a high school diploma or its equivalent is required. Some Educational Opportunity Programs can also help you obtain a high school equivalency diploma.

Another way you can obtain college credits and even earn a college degree is through **Regents College**. Regents College is a non-profit educational service organization offering external degree programs for adults. You can receive college credits and a degree by taking exams which cover undergraduate, college-level course work in the following areas: Liberal Arts, Technology, Business, Education and Nursing. The Regents College examinations allow you to achieve recognition no matter how or where you've obtained your knowledge.

Regents College is accredited by the Commission of Higher Education, Middle States Association of Colleges and Schools. The Nursing programs are accredited by the National League for Nursing. Regents College programs are registered with the New York State Education Department. You do not have to be a resident of New York in order to enroll in a program and Regents programs are available worldwide. You can also receive college credit through Regents Examinations for prior business and industrial training, military service, education and special assessment.

Many colleges and universities in New York and other states recognize Regents College Examinations for credit or advanced standing. I have personally taken several Regents College Exams and received 18 credits to fulfill certification requirements for New York State. These credits also qualified me for a salary differential at work and were applied toward my masters degree. Needless to say, Regents exams have saved me a considerable amount of time and money.

If you would like to learn more about Regents College examinations, you can receive a brochure and free copies of study guides by requesting them directly from: Regents College, 7 Columbia Circle Albany, NY 12203 (518) 464-8500. Or, log onto: **www.regents.edu**.

Virtual College

There is considerable talk about "Distant Education", obtaining a college degree online by taking courses from what is called a "Virtual College". Many of the large name colleges are now offering a number of Distant Education programs, NYU, Duke, University of Maine and Georgia Institute of Technology among them. The **U.S. Dept. of Education**'s website **www.ed.gov** has a listing of accredited colleges, many of which offer online courses and degrees. Or, call: (888) 445-7745 for more information.

If you decide to attend a traditional college, the earlier you consider your choices, the better. High school juniors should begin writing college admissions offices for information and applications. High school guidance counselors are there to help, but don't rely on them entirely. Do your own research. Log onto:

www.collegeboard.org • www.embark.com
www.collegequest.com

There are a number of guides to colleges. Review as many as you can. Barron's, U.S. News and World Report, Peterson's and Lovejoy's are popular sources of information. The time and energy you invest in learning about a school will be well worth it.

Apply as early as possible, to as many schools as possible. Your odds of being accepted will increase with an early application. Approach the application process seriously. Unless the college conducts interviews, your application is the only thing that will represent you. Make a copy of the application and use it as your rough draft. Check grammar and spelling and have someone proofread the rough draft before filling out the actual application.

If feasible, visit the school(s) you are considering and peruse their websites. Choosing a college is a very important decision, one that will amount to years of dedicated study. The decision you make now will affect you your entire lifetime.

Following is a listing of historically Black Colleges. This is only a brief listing. The schools offer many other programs than those noted. If you are interested in a particular college, call the admissions office and ask them to send you a brochure or email them through their websites. Schools that are members of the United Negro College Fund are noted with a "✔". If you enroll in any of the UNCF schools and show financial need, you may be eligible for the many scholarship programs UNCF offers.

Historically Black Colleges and Universities

Alabama A&M University: Food and Crop Research, Teacher Education. (256) 851-5245

Arkansas at Pine Bluff (University of): BA, BS, Nursing, Law and Medical School. (807) 543-8000

Barber-Scotia College, North Carolina: Pre-med, Math, Business, Computer, Liberal Arts. (704) 789-2900 ✔

Benedict College, South Carolina: Teaching, Health Careers. (803) 253-5143 – www.bchome.benedict.edu ✔

Bennett College, North Carolina: Biology, Chemistry, Teaching, Music, Mass Communications. (336) 370-8624 www.bennett.edu ✔

Bethune-Cookman College, Florida: Liberal Arts, Humanities and Nursing. (800) 448-0228 www.bethune.cookman.edu ✔

Bowie State University, Maryland: Liberal Arts and Sciences. (301) 464-6570

Central State University, Ohio: Water Resources Management, Engineering. (937) 376-6348

Claflin College, South Carolina: Occupational and Physical Therapy, Radiation Technology, Engineering. (803) 535-5097 www.icusc.org/claflin/cchome.htm ✔

Clark Atlanta University, Georgia: Political Science, Business, Communication Arts and Math. (404) 880-6605 www.cau.edu ✔

Coppin State College, Maryland: Nursing, Management Science, Education. (410) 383-5990

Delaware State college: Business, Liberal Arts, Nursing, Pre-Law and Pre-Med. (302) 739-4914/4918

Dillard University, Louisiana: Business, Science, Communications and Nursing. (504) 286-4670 www.dillard.edu ✔

District of Columbia (University of): Liberal and Fine Arts, Human Ecology, Business, Life and Physical Sciences. (202) 274-5000

Edward Waters College, Florida: Health and Physical Education, Communications, Business and Science. (904) 366-2506 – www.ewc.edu ✔

Fisk University, Tennessee: Pre-Professional Studies, Physics, Pre-Med, Pharmacy, Dental, Law, Engineering. (615) 329-8666 – www.fisk.edu ✔

Florida A&M University: (850) 599-3796 call for university catalog.

Florida Memorial College, Miami: Accounting, Biology, Chemistry, Education and Business management. (305) 626-3745 – www.fmc.edu ✔

Grambling State University: Nursing, Law and a number of other programs. (318) 274-2435

Hampton University, Virginia: (757) 727-5328 call for catalog.

Howard University, Washington DC: Over 200 subjects with doctorates in many areas. (202) 806-2650

Huston-Tillotson College, Texas: BA, BS, Computer Science, Hotel/Restaurant Management, Mass Communications. (800) 321-7421 ✔

Interdemoninational Theological Center, Georgia: Bible, Christian Education, Church History, World Religions, Homiletics. (404) 527-7790 ✔

Jackson State University, Mississippi: Computer Science, Mass Communication. (601) 968-2100

Jarvis Christian College, Texas: Sociology, Accounting, Music, Marketing. (903) 769-2174 ✔

Johnson C. Smith University, North Carolina: Biology, Business, Chemistry, Psychology, Computers, Communication Arts. (800) 782-7303 – www.jcsu.edu ✔

Kentucky State University: Bachelor of Arts, Bachelor of Science, Nursing. (502) 227-6813

Knoxville College, Tennessee: Business, Education, Social Service, Performing Arts, Math, Humanities. (423) 524-6511

Lane College, Tenessee: Biology, Business, Chemistry, Criminal Justice, Computer studies. (800) 390-7533 www.lane-college.edu ✔

Langston University, Oklahoma: (405) 466-3428 call for catalog.

LeMoyne-Owen College, Tennessee: Pre-Nursing, Business and Liberal Arts. (901) 942-7302 ✔

Lincoln University, Missouri: Business Administration, Education, Nursing Science, Computer, Education. (573) 681-5599

Livingstone College, North Carolina: Law, Business Administration, Pharmacy, Engineering. (704) 638-5530 www.livingstone.edu ✔

Mary Holmes College, Mississippi: Liberal Arts transfer programs, Associate Degree Programs. (601) 494-6820

Miles College, Alabama: Accounting, Biology, Business Education, Communication. (800) 445-0708 www.miles.edu ✔

Morehouse College, Georgia: Political Science, Biology, Humanities, Liberal Arts and Science. (404) 215-2638 www.morehouse.edu ✔

Morgan State University, Maryland: Urban Studies, Arts, Sciences, Humanities. (493) 885-3000

Morris Brown College, Georgia: Humanities, Computer, Business Administration. (404) 220-0152 ✔

Morris College, South Carolina: Army ROTC, Media, Business Administration, Pre-law, Computers, Humanities. (888) 778-1345 www.icusc.org/morris/mchome.htm ✔

Norfolk State University, Virginia: High Technology and Business, Social Work and Research, Sciences. (757) 683-8396 ✔

Oakwood College, Alabama: Liberal Arts, Christian Living, Spiritual Living and Leadership. (256) 726-7000 www.oakwood.edu ✔

Paine College, Georgia: Liberal Arts, Health Sciences, Teacher Education. (706) 821-8320 – www.paine.edu ✔

Paul Quinn College, Texas: Chemical and Systems Technology, Engineering, Pre-Nursing, Liberal Arts and Sciences. (214) 302-3520 – www.pqc.edu ✔

Philander Smith College, Arkansas: Business Administration, Pre-Med, Business. (501) 370-5219 – www.philander.edu ✔

Prairie View A&M University, Texas: Engineering, Architecture, Agriculture, Natural Sciences, Nursing, Biology. (409) 857-2626

Rust College, Missouri: Mass Communications. (601) 252-8000 ✔

Saint Augustine's College, North Carolina: Liberal Arts. (919) 516-4014 ✔

Shaw University, North Carolina: Accounting, Biology, Business Mgmt, Education, Chemistry. (919) 546-8275 www.shawu.edu ✔

St. Paul's College, Virginia: Pre-Med, Math, Sociology, Education, Business Administration. (804) 848-3984 ✔

Sojourner-Douglass College, Maryland: Bachelor of Arts, Business Administration, Human Resources. (410) 276-0306

Southern University at New Orleans: Social Work and Natural Sciences. (504) 286-5314

Spelman College, Georgia: BA, BS, Liberal Arts. (404) 681-3643 www.spelman.edu ✔

Stillman College, Alabama: Science and Teacher Education, Law. (205) 349-4240 – www.stillman.edu ✔

Talladega College, Alabama: Biology, Busines and Finance. (800) 633-2440 ✔

Tennessee State University: Engineering, Technology, Allied Health and Communications, Nursing. (615) 963-5000

Texas College: BA, BS, Liberal Arts. (903) 593-8311

Tougaloo College, Mississippi: Art, Biology, Chemistry, Ecomonics, Psychology and Liberal Arts. (601) 977-7770 www.tougaloo.edu ✔

Tuskegee University, Alabama: Aerospace, Chemical and Electrical Engineering, Architecture, Veterinary Medicine, Pre-med, Biology, Agriculture. (800) 622-6531 – www.tusk.edu ✔

Virgin Islands, (University of the): St. Thomas: Marine Biology, Business and Liberal Arts. (340) 776-9200

Virginia State University: Agriculture, Education, Business, Accounting, Social Work. (804) 524-5902

Virginia Union University, Richmond: Accounting, Business, Music, Theology, Criminal Justice and Teaching. (804) 257-5855 www.vuu.edu ✔

Vorhees College, South Carolina: Criminal Justice, Computer, Business, Natural Science. (803) 793-3351 www.vorhees.edu ✔

West Virginia State College: Biology, Chemistry, Criminal Justice, Education, Business, Social Work. (304) 766-3221

Wilberforce University, Ohio: Sociology, Rehabilitation Counseling, Accounting, Liberal Arts. (800) 367-8568 www.wilberforce.edu ✔

Wiley College, Texas: Hotel & Restaurant Management, Pre-med, Biology, Business and Computer. (903) 927-3255 www.wiley.edu ✔

Xavier University of Louisiana: Pre-Med and Pharmacy. (504) 483-7388 – www.xuia.edu ✔

Need More Info?

The National Association for College Admissions Counseling has a free, brochure; *Guide for Parents*. Call: (703) 836-2222 or write: 1631 Prince Street, Alexandria, VA 22314-2818. Another good source of information may be the website: **www.black-collegian.com**.

Need a Lift? College Financial Aid Handbook, published by The American Legion. National Emblem Sales, P.O. Box 1050, Indianappolis, IN 46206 (317) 630-1200. Cost: $3.00.

Don't Miss Out: The Ambitious Student's Guide to Financial Aid, Octameron Association (703) 836-5480. Cost: $8.00.

Paying for College: A Guide for Parents, published by The College Board. (800) 323-7155. Cost: $14.95.

Are you being Tested?

Planning to take exams such GRE, GMAT, TOEFL and PRAXIS? Educational Testing Service's free *Educational Testing Service Publications Catalog* lists publications and prices. (609) 771-7243 **www.ets.org/store.html**

www.gedtest.org (GED Preparation) Get info on the test.

www.back2college.com Adult education clearinghouse.

www.ask.com (Ask Jeeves) Ask a question literally about anything. Really!

www.netlibrary.com (Net Library) Internet-based library, electronic books. Free reading and download e-books.

Another Page in my Personal Chapter...

Mind over matter. Your body, your brain. Write what you wish. Use the pen to release positive emanations. Suggestions: What are my goals now? How can I achieve them? How do I perceive myself? Where should I focus the most energy?

_____

_____

_____

_____

_____

_____

_____

_____

_____

_____

_____

_____

_____

_____

This is YOUR personal page. Write on! ✎ *More space on the reverse...*

Road Warrior
Conquering The World, One Trip at a Time.

 If you're like many women who have *Delilah Power!* you possess an insatiable curiosity about the Earth. You know the world is broader than the neighborhood you live in and you want to learn more about it. While some of us never get the chance to travel to the farthest reaches of the globe, others embark on journey after journey in search of life's answers. What these women discover is often surprising, enlightening and immensely fulfilling.

Imagine visiting the great pyramids of Egypt and Nubia which were built by our magnificent African ancestors, touching stone and sand and connecting with your incredible heritage. Picture yourself eating your favorite Chinese food in China, or french fries in Paris. What would it be like to cruise the languid rivers of Venice in a gondola, visit ancient Greek temples and watch a roaring bullfight in Spain? There's a whole world without limits waiting for you.

Take a minute to think about someplace in the world you've always wanted to visit. If you had the money right now to travel anywhere in the world you wanted, where would it be? In the chapter *Money Madness*, I talk about a two-dollar a day strategy that can help you save hundreds of dollars a year. If you were to follow the strategy and other money saving tips mentioned, you might afford a dream vacation within a few months. What better way to celebrate your independence than to succumb to wanderlust and explore the world?

Traveling doesn't have to be expensive. Sure, we'd all love to go first class and enjoy the amenities such luxury brings, but the reality is, most of us are on a tight budget. This chapter attempts to provide you with helpful information for traveling safely and on the cheap. Because you have *Delilah Power!* you know how to shop conscientiously and make the most of your money. In addition to the websites listed herein, you'll access information on traveling and vacationing for free. What? No kidding!

Discount Travel Companies

Throughout the country, thousands of hotel rooms and airline seats go unoccupied everyday. This is why so many travel agents and companies are able to offer you low and discounted fares. Many of these companies can be accessed via the internet and will book trips for you online. If you don't have a computer, visit your local library. Most public libraries have computers available for public use. You'll probably have to sign a waiting list or reserve a station in advance.

Vacation and Personal Pleasure

www.astanet.com (American Society of Travel Agents) Directory of travel companies and travel agents. Hotspots, Forums, Links, Travel Info, Scholarships, Travel Careers, Educational Seminars.

www.earthcam.com See events around the world, live! Also: Arts & Entertainment, Business, Space & Science, Society & People, Sports & Recreation, Education and more.

www.epicurious.com (Conde Nast Traveler) Sign up with several of the major airlines' email notification programs for last minute bargain fares.

www.insideflyer.com Deals for frequent flyers. www.webflyer.com.

www.lonelyplanet.com Collection of travel links called *subwwway*. Also featured: Propaganda, Destinations, The Scoop, eKno,

www.oanda.com (The Currency Site) Features: Oanda Converter which calculates the value of the U.S. dollar in 164 foreign currencies. Print out a conversion sheet to take on your trip. Historical tables, forecasts for world currencies, find a loan.

www.priceline.com (Priceline.com) Name your price for airline tickets and hotel rooms, home mortgages, home equity loans, mortgage financing, new cars and trucks.

www.traveldiscounters.com Wholesale airline tickets, guarantee of $50-$150 off domestic fares above $300.

www.traveler.net Travel advice including: Top 10 Travel Tips.

Business-Related Travel

www.biztravel.com (Biztravel.com) You can book a business trip or vacation, plan a meeting, charter a flight and more.

www.expedia.msn.com (MSN Expedia) Book flights, reserve hotel rooms and rental cars. Look for Special Deals, Fare Compare, Sports & Adventure, Customer Support and more.

www.previewtravel.com (Preview Travel) Contains vacation, Car & Restaurant Finder, Video Gallery, Travel Newswire and Travel Store.

www.thetrip.com (The Trip.com) Access Flight tracker, Newsstand, Marketplace and more. Also see: Business Class Deals.

www.travelocity.com (Travelocity.com) This site features: Travel Tools, Special Offers, Traveler's Investment Center and Flight Paging. Free membership.

To book flights and vacations with the major airlines directly, try logging onto their websites. You may receive special discounts for booking online. You also save time bypassing a visit to a travel agent.

www.americanairlines.com (American Net SAAvers)

www.delta-air.com (Delta Special Offers)

www.flycontinental.com (C.O.O.L Travel Specialists)

www.northwestairlines.com (Northwest Cybersavers)

www.twa.com (TWA Hot Deals)

www.ual.com (United E-Fares)

www.usair.com (US Airways E-Savers)

Note: Under federal law, airlines must compensate you for unreasonable delays in your flight. During peak travel seasons, airlines often overbook their flights to ensure full seating. This can cause considerable confusion, frustration and aggravation for passengers. If you don't raise a big fuss, the airline will wait as long as possible before offering you any compensation. Your course of action: complain from start to finish. In the event you are unduly inconvenienced by an airline, insist on more than an apology. Insist on monetary compensation. In all likelihood, you'll get it.

Free Vacationing

Feel like vacationing for free? How is that possible? Become a volunteer! You can take a "volunteer vacation" so that all of your expenses (considered contributions) in relation to the services you provide are fully tax deductible. Ultimately, your airfare to the site, lodging, meals and equipment cost you nothing and you've had the adventure of a lifetime.

Earthwatch, a non-profit organization, allows you to work with prominent researchers in a range of field expeditions. Expeditions are located in some of the most exotic places around the world and involve working with plants and animals, exploring shipwrecks, learning archaeology and more. You can apply for an Earthwatch Expedition Award to cover some or all of your costs.

Earthwatch
680 Mt. Auburn Street, Box 403, Watertown, Massachusetts 02272
(617) 926-8200 www.earthwatch.org

Other travel opportunities are available through the **University Research Expeditions Program** (UREP). Participate in field expeditions all over the world:

University Research Expeditions Program, University of California
Berkeley, CA 94720-7050 (510) 642-6585

Another possibility to explore is the Archaeological Institute of America. Call or write and ask for the *Archaeological Fieldwork Opportunities Bulletin.*

Archaeological Institute of America, Boston University
656 Beacon Street, Boston, MA 02215-6550 (617) 353-9361

Operation Crossroads Africa conducts programs in Africa, the Caribbean and United States. Volunteers can participate in short-term community development projects. Fund raising counseling can help applicants raise funds to cover the participation fee.

Operation Crossroads Africa (OCA)
475 Riverside Drive, New York, NY 10115 (212) 870-2106

If you enjoy the wilderness and want to do your part to preserve and manage the environment, you might appreciate volunteering in a U.S. national park or forest. You can offer your services in a range of areas such as monitoring wildlife, planting trees, photography, computers and more. Write to the following three agencies and ask for a listing of their locations.

National Parks Listing
The National Parks Service Office of Information
1849 C Street NW Washington, DC 20240

U.S. Department of Agriculture Forest Service
Washington DC 20250

Division of Refuges, U.S. Fish and Wildlife Service
441 North Fairfax Drive, Arlington, VA 22203
(703) 358-1744

Are you an educator interested in volunteer teaching opportunities abroad? Contact:

AFT International Affairs Department
222 New Jersey Avenue, NW Washington DC 20001-2079

Teachers on Volunteer Service in Israel (TOVS)
110 East 59th Street, New York, NY 10022 (212) 339-6917

You can also take the New World Teachers TEFL Certificate Course to teach English in a foreign country. No prior teaching experience required.

New World Teachers
1027 10th Street, 4th Floor Sacramento, CA 95814
(800) 644-5424/(916) 445-3428

WorldTeach
30 JFK, Cambridge, MA 02138 (617) 495-5527

National Association for Foreign Student Affairs (NAFSA)
1307 NW New York Ave, Washington, DC 20009 (202) 737-3699

International Travel for Teachers and Students

EF Educational Tours
One Memorial Drive, Cambridge, MA 02142 (800) 637-8222

International Universities
766 West 23rd Street, San Pedro, CA 90731 (800) 547-5678

CIEE Work Abroad
205 East 42nd Street, New York, NY 10017

IST Global Talent Search / Youth in Action, Inc.
4848 Laveview Avenue, Yorba Linda, CA 92886
(714) 777-4373/(714) 779-7392

For details on the Fulbright U.S. Student Program as well as scholarships, fellowships and grants for study and work abroad, contact:

Institute of International Education
809 United Nations Plaza, New York, NY 10017 (212) 883-8200

Other travel Opportunities

Become an air courier. Act as an on-board freelance air courier for an international freight company. Fly at a discounted rate or free. One such company:

Air Courier Association
191 University Blvd. Suite 300, Denver CO 80206
(303) 279-3600

Business executives and managers have opportunities to spend time in Russia Ukraine, Romania, Georgia and Azerbaijan as a volunteer advisor to small and medium-sized businesses.

Citizens Democracy Corps
1400 I Street, NW, Suite 1125, Washington, DC 20005
www.cdc.org (800) 394-1945

Safe and Sound

Road warriors take precautions to ensure their safety while traveling, If you follow these simple tips and exercise care in your venture, you'll have the adventure of a lifetime. It's time to enjoy yourself. Bon voyage!

- If visiting a foreign country, know where the U.S. Consulate and Embassy are before arriving. Also locate an American Express office, if possible.

- While visiting a foreign country, familiarize yourself with its laws and abide by them. Laws which protect you in the U.S. may not exist in other countries. In the event of an incident, your ignorance will be considered inexcusable.

- To prevent losing your passport while vacationing, make a copy of the first page to carry with you. Secure the actual passport in a location such as a hotel safe.

- Always check your hotel room for secure locks on the doors and windows. Don't leave your valuables unattended in the room. Utilize the hotel safe.

- Some countries require an International Driving Permit for driving. Contact your local AAA office for more information. The permit may cost under $20.

- Familiarize yourself with foreign currency before or as soon as you arrive in a foreign country. Convert money accurately in your mind (www.oanda.com).

- Avoid looking like a tourist. While site seeing, keep a close watch on your belongings and be wary of overly friendly people. Pickpockets know you're there to relax and spend money. If you're careless, they'll nail you.

- Know how to dial emergency numbers and contact authorities for assistance. Most of all, be ready to react to danger at all times.

- Become familiar with the social customs in a foreign country to avoid offending anyone. What may be acceptable behavior in the U.S. could be insulting in another culture.

The U.S. State Department Travel Information can supply you with the following: travel warnings, passport information, visa services, listing of U.S. Embassy and Consulate websites worldwide, links to other related sites and more. **http://travel.state.gov**.

The Office of American Citizens Services is an after-hours number for travel safety and emergencies such as Americans missing abroad, arrest, detention, death abroad, etc. Contact them at: (202) 647-5225.

The **Center for Disease Control** website has an area called Travelers Health, which gives a summary of health information for international travel. Vaccine recommendations, alerts of disease outbreaks and tips on how to protect yourself from diseases while traveling outside of the United States. www.cdc.gov or call: (800) 311-3435/(404) 639-3311/(404) 639-3534.

Traveling with your pet? Log onto: **www.takeyourpet.com**, **www.aspca.org/petcare/travel.htm** or **www.hua.org for helpful information**. Also log onto: **www.aaa.com**.

On a Roll!

Are you on a roll? If you've ever purchased or owned a vehicle, you've probably felt you were "taken for a ride" by unscrupulous salesmen and mechanics at some time or another. When certain men see a woman enter their repair shop or dealership, they assume she's an ideal target, unaware of what's going on and willing to pay whatever price they ask. There are many tactics they can use to swindle you, speaking to you in a condescending tone, or patronizing you in an attempt to placate you. If you begin to ask too many questions, they might fast talk you or lightly brush off your inquiry. Unfortunately, these tactics often work with many women. As a result, we either end up paying more for less or just paying too much, period.

Now that you have *Delilah Power!* however, all that is about to change. But first, complete this short checklist and test your auto savvy.

Auto Savvy Checklist
I can...

- ☐ check my tires and properly inflate them.
- ☐ fix a flat in an emergency.
- ☐ jump-start my battery using booster cables.
- ☐ check and add oil when necessary.
- ☐ check and add windshield washer fluid.
- ☐ check and add antifreeze.
- ☐ light an emergency flare.
- ☐ change a headlight or rear bulb.
- ☐ check and change the air filter.
- ☐ understand information my mechanic gives me about my car and repairs done.

I can identify...

- ❏ my car's engine.
- ❏ the carburetor.
- ❏ the alternator.
- ❏ all or most of the items under the hood.

I know...

- ❏ what emergency items to store in my trunk.*
- ❏ when I need an oil change and/or tune-up.
- ❏ the book value of my car/car I intend to buy.
- ❏ how to research a vehicle's title.
- ❏ which dealerships in my area are reputable.
- ❏ which features are standard in a new car and which are extra.

16-20 checked: Fantastic job! You've got real auto savvy! You're probably prepared for an auto emergency and know how to handle yourself on the road. I'll bet you save quite a bit on auto repairs and purchases. Your knowledge is impressive and you're obviously a powerful and independent lady. Congratulations! *A+*

11-15 checked: Great job! You know quite a bit about your car and are probably very independent. You'll also make fairly wise decisions when purchasing a vehicle. As there is always more to learn, you want to continue asking questions and using your smarts. *B+*

6-10 checked: You have some knowledge, but could be more involved with your vehicle. You know the basics and probably don't hesitate to ask questions, but you could investigate more. Be careful when taking your car to an unfamiliar auto shop. If you are planning to purchase a new car or take a long road trip, pull out the manuals and study. You've got more learning to do. *C+*

---

* Flares, a working spare tire, a blanket, jumper cables, a first-aid kit, water, oil, antifreeze, windshield washer fluid, an auto tool kit, a jack, flat-fix foam.

0-5 checked: You could be an ideal target for unscrupulous car salesmen and mechanics. You may be a bit too trusting, or you may rely too heavily on someone else to take care of your business. There is no real benefit in being dependent. You are not prepared for an auto emergency. It would be to your benefit to read this chapter carefully and take steps to learn more about your car. Avoid spending money on anything auto-related unless you really know what's going on. Your grade: *F*

Now that you've been quizzed on your auto savvy, let's talk a little about maintaining and repairing your car. After that, we'll discuss what makes a good mechanic, tips on buying a new or used car and auto leasing.

Preventive Medicine

If you drive into a repair shop, hand over your vehicle and fail to ask questions about the car or what repairs are needed, you've given the shop an open invitation to swindle you. Your best defense against a dishonest mechanic is to have general knowledge of your vehicle and practice preventive medicine.

Here are a few simple ways you can help your car run smoothly. These tips were given to me by a skilled and reputable mechanic.

- Get an oil change every three months or 3000 miles.

- Change gaskets, filters, sparkplugs, etc. according to the car manufacturer's specifications. The car's auto manual will tell you how often these things need to be changed. A calendar will help you remember.

- Always keep fluids at their proper levels. If you're not sure about your fluid levels, ask a mechanic.

- Avoid driving on a near-empty gas tank. This causes dirt to accumulate in the engine. Your best bet: put gas in when the meter drops to ¼ full.

- If your car makes strange noises or begins to drive funny, get it checked out immediately. A good idea would be to write down the car's symptoms. This might help your mechanic diagnose the problem.

- Keep tires properly inflated. Under-inflation causes excessive drag and over-inflation can cause a blow-out. Keeping tires properly inflated also saves gas.

What's a Good Mechanic?

A good mechanic is someone who will:

- Take time to answer your questions.
- Test drive your car before and after the repair.
- Show you the problem with your car and the actual repairs once completed.
- Not initiate a repair without your approval.
- Give you a written estimate if you request it, as well as a breakdown of the final bill.
- Guarantee his work.

A good mechanic will have received his training from a legitimate auto-mechanic school. If you ask about his credentials, he will not hesitate to tell you. There are mechanics who learn auto-repair on the street and will do patch jobs on your car for a great price. If your car is busted and you don't want to spend a lot of money, these mechanics may be for you. However, they make more mistakes and generally won't refund your money.

Always Check the Work!

Make sure you know what's going on every step of the way. You don't have to know a whole lot about cars in order to check repairs. All you need is some common sense. If something the mechanic says doesn't sound right, it probably isn't. Don't hesitate to question him.

Some sleazy mechanics will tamper with your car behind your back and insist you need additional repairs. One guy over-inflated my tires and said I would need eighteen hundred dollars worth of work. I wound up paying seventy-five dollars for a wheel alignment at another shop and my car was fine. Had I not double-checked, I would've been taken for a ride!

Hang around while getting your car repaired to see what work is being performed. Repair shops often post signs asking customers to stay out of the work area due to insurance regulations. However, a good mechanic will escort you in, show you the problem and the repair, including all visible replacement parts. If possible, stay with the mechanic as he fixes the car. You can use this time to ask questions and learn more about your car.

Double-check the work after the repair is done. When mechanics are very busy, they can become careless or forgetful. Mechanics have left tools under the hood of my car (once I found a wrench), forgotten to replace minor parts, etc. I had my car repaired at one shop and found chicken bones under the hood when I got home! Double-checking serves dual purposes: you see where your money went and you can remind the mechanic of any minor details he may have missed.

Here's another tip: if possible, have a man accompany you to either drop off or pick up your car. Mechanics respect so-called male authority, perhaps because they risk physical confrontation if they mess around. If you take your car for repairs alone, dress attractively. Mechanics often go the extra mile for attractive ladies. All you have to do is smile sweetly, feign helplessness and give him a little tip for the extra work. In other words, capitalize on his sexist attitude. Get yours, Girl!

Purchase or Lease?

So, you're ready for a new car. Getting a new car can be an exciting experience. The question is, would it be better to purchase a new car or lease it? Either choice is a major financial decision with distinct benefits and drawbacks. Because you have *Delilah Power!* you can effectively consider your options before deciding.

Advantages of Purchasing

- You can take pride in ownership.
- You establish equity in your vehicle.
- You can customize your vehicle without getting permission from the lessor and without violating a lease agreement.
- You are not restricted to low-mileage driving.
- If you purchase your vehicle outright, you can avoid paying interest on financing. You also have flexibility regarding the type of insurance policy you take out (liability as opposed to full coverage).

The Flipside:

- You will be fully responsible for maintenance and repairs once your warranty expires.
- You have to deal with trading the car in or selling it when you're ready to make a new purchase.
- The car is a depreciable asset which will decrease in value as time goes on.

Leasing a Vehicle

Car Dealers encourage leasing because they know you'll be back when the lease is up. In order to qualify for leasing, you must be in good standing with the credit bureaus. Leasing a car can be a complicated process. Before attempting to lease a car, you should find out as much as possible about consumer laws in your state which may protect you. You should also seek legal advice. If you're not careful, you could wind up paying much more for the lease than you should.

Advantages of Leasing

- You can drive an extravagant car for less than if you purchased it.
- You can drive a new car every few years.
- Your car will be covered by a warranty for as long as you drive it.
- You don't have to be bothered with selling or trading in a used car.
- There are tax benefits if you lease a car for business purposes.

The Flipside:

- Your car payments go on forever.
- At lease end, there is no trade-in value which you can apply to another car you may want to purchase.
- You face stiff penalties if you try to terminate the lease early.
- You will be charged for putting high mileage on the vehicle.
- You will be charged for damage that isn't considered normal "wear and tear".

If you are seriously considering leasing a car, you may find it helpful to contact your state Attorney General and ask if your state has a vehicle lease disclosure law such as the **Motor Vehicle Retail Leasing Act** in New York. A law such as this gives consumers important legal rights and will protect you before, during and at the end of your lease. Also ask the Attorney General's office if they have a consumer guide to automobile leasing. The guide should explain the leasing process in detail, spell out your rights and responsibilities as a lessee and answer any questions you may have.

New York State Attorney General Information and complaint hotline: (800) 771-7755.

Once you've negotiated a favorable lease, you will sign what is called a *purchase offer form.* This makes your lease offer official, and a manager will sign it to accept your offer on the dealer's behalf. Do not confuse this with the actual leasing contract. Make certain all terms of the lease are spelled out in the purchase offer form exactly as when you calculated the lease payment.

Watch out for the fine print in the contract, such as a high down payment, low mileage allowance, a huge disposition fee, high fees for early termination or if you want to buyout, the addition of credit-life, accident or health insurance without your request or permission and high security deposits. Review all details carefully.

☞ Do not sign anything unless you fully understand it!

☞ Do not sign any binding legal document without seeking competent legal advice beforehand!

Buying a New Car

When buying a new car, ignorance will cost you. Control your excitement, think reasonably and take your time. If you purchase in haste, you may spend more than you need to.

Decide on the type of vehicle you want to purchase, rather than shop randomly. Once you know what you want, you can do your homework. Learn as much as possible about the car before you go into a dealership.

Research the vehicle by reading automotive publications such as *Car & Driver, Motor Trend,* etc.

Next, consider where you might purchase the vehicle. Evaluate different dealerships. I spoke with a gentleman who worked for a large-name dealership for many years. He offered these suggestions:

- Check out the business practices of each dealership, large chains included. Call the Better Business Bureau in the city where the dealership is located to find out if there are a large number of complaints registered against the business. The Better Business Bureau has a website which may be of help: **www.bbb.org**.

- If you purchase from a huge dealership, be prepared for possible confusion and aggravation. You may go through a number of people and departments each time you need service.

- Never shop at a dealership late in the day, or when you're tired. Shop in the morning, or when you feel energetic. Give yourself several hours to browse. If you become overwhelmed, stop, withdraw and take a 24 hour break. You'll make wiser choices and avoid buying out of frustration.

- *You* dictate what salesman sells you the car and when the negotiations begin. Remember, it's your money and the dealership needs you much more than you need it. If you don't like the vibe, exit.

- Once you've chosen a salesman, find out more about him. You'll want a knowledgeable salesman with a long history of sales.

- Car salesmen understand human nature. So, avoid giving out personal information. Once salesmen know your lifestyle, driving habits, tastes, etc., they tailor their sales pitches to seduce you.

- The salesman intends to sell you the priciest car with the most luxurious options. Dealers make the bulk of their money from options. Don't buy options you don't want. Make it clear you'll buy elsewhere if they try to force options on you.

• Don't allow a car dealer to charge you extra money for features that are required by law (such as seatbelts) or standard (such as carpeting) from the car manufacturer.

• The cost of preparing your car for delivery is already included in the manufacturer's price.

• Make sure every option you purchase contains the manufacturer's label. This way, the dealership is responsible for these options, should they break.

• Understand the terms of the sales contract and argue as many of the dealer's charges as possible. "DAP, Locator Cost and Procurement Cost" are all charges that are negotiable.

• Test drive the car for as long as you feel necessary. Don't let the salesman rush you in any way. If you feel you're being pressured, calmly walk out.

Purchasing a Used Car

Did you know... A vehicle that has been declared unroadworthy in one state can be sold with a clean title in another? When you purchase a used car, even from a dealer, you run the risk of purchasing a problem. What can you do to minimize that risk?

Carfax is an independent company which maintains a vehicle history database of over 600 million vehicles. For a fee, they will perform a computerized background check on the car you want to buy and provide you with a printed report by fax. You give them the Vehicle Identification Number (VIN) which is usually located on the dashboard near the windshield, or on the driver side door. Within an hour, Carfax faxes you a report on the title. Carfax can help you reduce the risk of buying a lemon by telling you where and when the vehicle was registered throughout its history and if the odometer readings show discrepancies. You will also find out whether the car has any of the following titles:

Salvage/Junk Title
Rebuilt/Reconstructed Title
Flood Damage Title
Damage Disclosure Title
Manufacturer Buyback (LEMON) Title

What does all of this mean? To sum it up, these titles indicate something may be seriously wrong with the car. In other words, forget about buying it! As of the date of this printing, a Carfax report costs $29.95 and includes what they call a "clean title history guarantee". For more information on the guarantee and their services: **Carfax** (800) 346-3846 / (800) 274-2277 **www.carfax.com**.

You can also research the title and obtain a similar report from a company called **Consumers Car Club** located at: 221 Main Street, Suite 250, San Francisco, CA 94105 (800) 227-2582.

Check out the *Consumer Reports Buying Guide* which has a large section on used cars. You can review re-liability reports for the type of car you'd like to buy.

Whether you buy a used car from a dealer, superstore or an individual, always ask for maintenance records (or receipts) for oil changes, radiator flushes, tune-ups and other maintenance suggested by the manufacturer. Have a good mechanic test drive the vehicle with you and look it over. Get in the car and make sure all doors, windows and controls work properly. Make sure all knobs and fixtures are securely attached. Check seat belts, front and back. Make sure stereo and speakers work properly. Examine the body closely, bumper to bumper, to see if the vehicle has been in a major accident. Run your hands over the car. Any lumps and bumps beneath surface paint may indicate patch work.

Used Car Superstores and Cyberdealers

Many people are purchasing used cars from "used car superstores". These stores provide haggle-free shopping and can probably supply you with whatever vehicle you want. The superstores inspect the vehicles they sell. However, as superstores get their cars from a range of sources, you'd still want to thoroughly investigate a vehicle before you buy it. Two superstores to contact:

CarMax: Schamburg, IL (888) 412-2629
AutoNation USA: (800) 288-6872

Cyberdealers have websites at which you can identify the type of vehicle you want to buy, configure it, get a quote and schedule a test drive. This is a new method of car buying, so do your research. Log on to Kelley Blue Book's website: **www.kbb.com**. KBB lists every vehicle and configuration of options possible to buy. Dealer invoice information is free.

After buying a used car, keep all repair receipts and maintain a record of problems you experience. This will benefit you if you need to return it to a dealer under the lemon law. If you're planning to sell or trade in a used car, don't fix any major mechanical problems or have body work done. Just organize repair receipts, clean the car thoroughly and give it a general maintenance check.

Roll On!

It's a great feeling to be in control of your life. This is what *Delilah Power!* is all about. Now that you have auto savvy, the only ride you'll get taken for in the future is one you choose to take!

AAA Automotive/Consumer Info: (800) 222-4357 **www.aaa.com**
U.S. Dept. of Transportation: (202) 366-4000
www.nhtfa.gov (800) 327-4263
Auto Safety Hotline: (202) 366-0123

Square Biz

Is there an Entrepreneur in You?

Complete this checklist to see if you have what it takes to be an entrepreneur and start your own business.

I, _____ believe that I am...

☐ an independent thinker.

☐ able to get along with different personalities.

☐ organized and good at planning.

☐ disciplined.

☐ able to complete projects.

☐ able to exercise sound judgment.

I can be...

☐ creative and imaginative.

☐ a motivated woman.

☐ determined whenever I set a goal.

☐ ambitious.

☐ optimistic.

☐ good at making decisions.

☐ willing to take risks.

☐ willing to learn what I don't know.

☐ someone who refuses to accept failure.

☐ calm, cool and collected in a crisis.

In addition, I have...

- ☐ physical and emotional stamina.
- ☐ the ability to visualize what I want.
- ☐ confidence in my abilities.
- ☐ ideas for making money.
- ☐ means to raise capital or money to invest.

Guess what? If you checked only one item on this list, you may have what it takes to become an entrepreneur. Sound unbelievable? Read on. People from all walks of life are starting businesses, becoming their own bosses, making money and enjoying financial independence. Many do it without previous business experience or a college degree. Why can't you?

The more items you've checked, the more equipped you are at present to undertake a business venture. The items left unchecked are simply skills which can be developed and learned. Because you have *Delilah Power!* you expect challenges in life and always rise to meet them. Here's a good place to start preparing yourself for a life of financial independence. Get the *Square Biz* on running your own company in this chapter. Read on!

Taking the Plunge

Going into business for yourself can be a rewarding experience. If your business becomes successful, you'll take pride in accomplishing your goals and achieving financial freedom. Owning a business can also be very stressful, but the pros eventually outweigh the cons.

Unfortunately, some women who are interested in entrepreneurialship have not had the opportunity to study business administration, or receive solid advice from a successful business owner. This and financial hardship can discourage a Black woman from pursuing a lifelong dream. If you have dreams of owning and managing a business, don't let a lack of knowledge or money deter you. With will and determination, you can make your dreams reality.

There are a number of things to think about: what product or service will you offer? Will you go solo or will you have partners? How much will it cost to set up your business? Where will you obtain the start-up capital? What supplies will you need and how will you manage financially if the business loses money or fails? What will you do to keep the business open if you or a relative becomes ill? If you plan to manufacture a product, you'll need to contact the Department of Buildings in your county before setting up shop to ensure you're in compliance with county zoning regulations.

If you fail to plan, you are ultimately planning to fail.

Poor planning is a major reason small businesses fail. Before you spend a dime, explore the viability of your business idea by drafting a business plan or outline. In addition to helping you organize, a business plan is needed to obtain money from other sources. Here's an outline of initial steps to start a business.

First Steps

1. Decide on the type of business.
2. Choose 3 possible names for the business.
3. Figure out your finances.
4. Decide on the legal structure of the business.
5. Write out a business plan.
6. Obtain a license/certificate for the business.
7. Obtain an Employer Identification Number.
8. Open a business bank account.
9. Get a P.O. Box.
10. Register as a sales tax vendor.
11. Obtain a DUNS number.
12. Obtain business insurance.

This chapter also lists resources which can help you with your business venture by saving you time and money. More on business plans will also be discussed. Sort through the information carefully and don't hesitate to seek outside help. Without a lot of dollars to spend, there's only one way to reach your goal: legwork.

If you have a large amount of venture capital at your disposal, you'll already be searching for a business location and considering other issues. You'll have a lawyer, accountant, advisor and other people to assist you. You probably won't step foot in a library, or file any forms on your own behalf. Chances are, your business will be up and running before one could say the words; 'make money'. Wouldn't it be great to start out that way? Since most of us don't have a lot of cash to toss around, we'll approach starting a business from the average woman's perspective. For now, let's look at those steps I mentioned previously in detail.

1. **Decide on the type of business** you want to start. This is pretty fundamental. What do you want to do, what product(s) will you sell?

2. **Choose three different names** for your business. When you attempt to register or incorporate your business, your first name choice may not be available. Suggestion: select names which reflect your company image or product.

3. **Figure out how much money you have** at your disposal for the initial investment and your projected ongoing expenses for the first two years. Experts say the first two years of operation are the most difficult for small businesses. You may not be able to predict where money will come from each week as you establish your corporate presence. This is when a business plan becomes most essential.

4. **Decide on the legal structure** (Sole Proprietorship, Partnership, Corporation) of your business. Each of these legal structures has advantages and disadvantages. Check with an attorney or accountant for more information on the type of business entity that would best suit your needs.

5. **Write out a rough business plan** or buy business plan software if you have a computer and begin creating a blueprint of your business.

6. **Obtain the necessary license or certificate** from the appropriate authority (County Clerk for Sole Proprietorship, Secretary of State to form a Corporation). Each state has particular regulatory requirements regarding businesses. Check with your state's **Department of Commerce** or Small Business Office for publications on licenses and permits in your state. These publications are usually free of charge.

U.S. Chamber of Commerce
1615 H. Street, N.W. Washington, DC 20062
(202) 659-6000 **www.uschamber.org**

If you decide to start a **sole proprietorship or partnership**, you may be able to register the business *yourself* with the County Clerk. The forms you'll need are often found at a stationary or business supply store. You make a personal trip to the County Clerk's office and do a name search to ensure no other business in the county has the same name as yours. Once the search is completed, you file the appropriate paperwork, pay a fee and are issued two certified copies of the Business Certificate (which you will display at your place of business and use to open a business bank account).

Fees to establish a sole-proprietorship or partnership vary from county to county. In New York for example, filing a Business Certificate costs about $120. Before you open a business bank account, obtain an Employer Identification Number (EIN). See item 7 for more information.

Solo or Duo?

If you decide to operate a sole proprietorship, you'll be in ultimate control of the business: a one-woman show in every way. You'll make all key decisions and benefit from all profits. You can sell or dissolve the business whenever you want and restructure the business at any time to suit your needs. The cost to set up and maintain a sole proprietorship is low and if you decide to pull out, you can do so with little difficulty.

You will however be liable for all debts and obligations of the business, including lawsuits. Personal assets and credit rating will be unprotected. Insurance can help, but a person who sues your business will ultimately be suing you. Many people thus choose to incorporate their businesses to shield themselves from liability. More information on incorporating a business follows later.

What about a partnership? Many people entering a partnership believe friendship will make the business work. However, your personal relationship with your partner may be the least important consideration. Sure, you want to work with someone you trust, but best friends don't always make the best business partners. There are a number of things to evaluate before you decide on such a venture.

In a business partnership, each partner will invest money, contribute property, labor or skills, and share profits and losses. As with a sole proprietorship, each individual will be personally liable for the obligations of the business, including lawsuits and debts. **Have a written agreement with your partner** including a buy out clause and outline your duties, responsibilities and anything else you can think of. Do this *before* you invest any real money. It would benefit you to consult with an attorney before entering into an agreement to protect yourself. Although not required by law, an agreement in writing could eliminate a number of difficulties in the future. Should you decide against a written agreement, check to see if your state has a partnership law. If so, such a law will set forth the rights and duties of both partners in absence of a written agreement.

A corporation on the other hand, is more expensive to form and to maintain. The benefits however, make it worthwhile for many business owners. Incorporation is done through the Department of State office. The main purpose of forming a corporation is to protect your personal assets if you're sued. The filing fee to incorporate your business can vary. As of this date, the filing fee for New York State for example, is $135 with a $10 fee for each additional certified copy you request. Other states cost considerably less. A name search must be done to ensure the name you've chosen is not being used anywhere else in the state. Many people hire lawyers to file the paperwork for them. Lawyers charge hundreds of dollars above the filing fee for their services, whatever amount they choose. Their services will usually include the filing fee, name search and a *Corporate Kit* for your company.

A **Corporate Kit** is a bundle of items you might need for your corporation: blank stock certificates, ledgers for your meetings (to take notes/minutes) and a rubber stamper called a corporate seal, similar to the seal a Notary Public uses. Some states, such as New York no longer require the use of a corporate kit. Call the **Division of Corporations** at the Department of State office in your state and inquire. You can also file the incorporation papers yourself. This may not be as complicated as you suspect and the Department of State may be able to supply you with the appropriate forms. You will probably need the help of an attorney however to set up your by-laws (rules the company and officers abide by) and to designate stocks to your partners or investors.

If you decide to use a lawyer to incorporate or for anything else, take your time and shop around for the best price. Unscrupulous people will always try to exploit your lack of knowledge to their advantage. Do your homework and don't let anyone pressure you into making a decision before you're ready. Since *you* are the one spending the money, you are in control. Be sure to get what you want and what you pay for. Always let a lawyer know that he is working for Y-O-U!

Once you've incorporated your business, you may file for what is called "S" status with the IRS. This status affords you specific tax benefits which an accountant can explain. Filing must be done within a certain amount of time after the date of incorporation, so investigate your options with a qualified professional before you set up the legal structure of your business.

7. **Obtain an Employer Identification Number (EIN)** from the IRS Department of the Treasury. This is a nine-digit number referred to a Tax I.D. number. You can apply for an EIN over the phone by calling: (800) 829-1040. If you use a lawyer to incorporate, he or she may be able to get the EIN for you. Establish your business bank account the EIN number. The EIN will ultimately identify your business in many of your transactions.

Even if you don't intend to have employees, get an EIN anyway. You'll be required to file quarterly tax forms for Social Security Tax withholding, but the forms are fairly simple to complete since you have no employees. If you hire people later on and have a payroll, your accountant can complete the forms for you.

8. **Open a bank account** in the name of the business. Most banks require a copy of your business license or Certificate of Incorporation as proof that the business legitimately exists before opening an account for you. Shop the banks for the best rates before opening an account. Commercial banks tend to be more impersonal and expensive, but will have better customer and merchant services. Smaller banks are usually community-based and have better rates, but may lack the customer service or account features you desire. Consider: How many locations does the bank have in your area and are they "small business friendly"? Does the bank offer merchant services such as credit card processing and are they set up for e-commerce? If you plan to have your own website and accept credit cards online for your products, you'll need a bank with e-commerce capability. We'll discuss e-commerce and web sites later. Warning: Once you open a businesses bank account, use the account solely for business purposes.

9. **Obtain a Postal Box.** Due to extensive mail-order fraud, the Post Office asks for a copy of your business license before issuing a box under a business name.

10. **Call your state's Department of Taxation.** You may be required to file specific forms and register as a sales tax vendor. Do this before making any sales. If you make taxable sales and neglect to file the proper forms with the state, you may be subject to substantial penalties. Ask the Department of Taxation how you can obtain a **Certificate of Authority** to collect sales tax in your state. This procedure may vary from state to state. You'll be required by law to collect sales tax from the customers in your state and pay the sales tax to the Department of Taxation.

11. **Obtain a DUNS Number**. A DUNS number is a nine-digit number issued by Dun & Bradstreet, a business information service. You might think of Dun & Bradstreet as a credit reporting agency for businesses, although they act in other

capacities. Dun & Bradstreet can assist you with other matters such as debt collection once your business is fully operational. When you call to sign up for your DUNS Number, a representative can fill you in on their many services. Although you are not legally obligated to apply for a DUNS Number, it may be to your advantage to do so. A DUNS Number gives your business credibility and lets others know you are serious. As your business grows, your D&B file will be updated and others can learn more about your company. When you create company correspondence, you can include your Tax I.D. and DUNS numbers. People who receive correspondence from you will feel confident you are legitimate.

Dun & Bradstreet
(800) 234-3867 Customer Service
(800) 333-0505 Reports Line and Self-Inquiry Line

12. **Obtain Business Insurance**. Business insurance is something you absolutely must have, especially if you will serve customers at your location and/or meet with clients. The type of insurance policies you'll need will depend on the kind of business you set up. For example, if you have a home-based business as many Americans do, you'll want to insure the equipment in your office. Many things can happen to your business records, computer and peripherals including fire, flood, theft and electrical surges. Your computer is also subject to hard drive failure and viruses. How will you be covered if valuable information is lost due to reasons beyond your control?

You'll also want liability insurance to cover potential injuries to clients and visitors who visit your location. A lawsuit, even a frivolous one, can cause financial ruin without proper insurance. If you own a home or work out of an apartment and already have homeowners insurance, see if your policy covers losses from business activities. It probably doesn't. If your business involves travel, you may need a policy to protect you and your inventory while away from the office such as, when making a delivery. What about insurance which covers you against crime? Insurance can be costly, but theft, disaster and lawsuits can destroy a life's worth of work. In short, better safe than sorry.

Following are two insurance companies which, as of this printing, offer In-Home Business policies. To locate others, check your phone book or local independent insurance agent. Comparison shop and choose an agent who's familiar with your industry. Assess your risks and buy the best protection you can afford. Review your policy carefully with your agent to be sure you're getting what you want for your money. Also see the listing of insurance related websites at the end of this chapter.

RLI Insurance Company, Illinois (309) 692-1000
CNA, Chicago (312) 822-5000 www.cna.com

One of the best resources available to you as a small business owner may be the **U.S. Small Business Administration** (SBA). The SBA has offices throughout the country and offers a range of programs and services including those geared for women and minorities. Receive help with applications to obtain loans, credit and more. Find out how you can become certified as a (8a) minority business and reap the benefits.

U.S. Small Business Administration
409 Third Street, S.W. Washington, DC 20416
1-800-8-ASK-SBA **www.sba.gov**

When contacting the Small Business Administration, be sure to ask about the following programs:

- **Minority Enterprise Development Program** Referred to as the 8(a) Program. This program provides for socially and economically disadvantaged businesses.
- **Service Corps of Retired Executives (SCORE)** National organization of business executives. Counseling, seminars and workshops, all free of charge.
- **Small Business Development Centers (SBDCs)** Training, assistance and counseling.
- **Small Business Institutes (SBIs)** Offices are located on college campuses. Counseling is offered by students and faculty to small business clients.
- **LowDoc** a low-documentation lending program for small businesses.

Elements of a Business Outline

I. **Name** of the business.

II. The actual or proposed **physical location**, including telephone and fax numbers (if available).

III. The **legal structure** of the business (corporation, sole-proprietorship, partnership).

IV. The **products/services** you will offer. How are your products or services unique? How does your company differ from the neighboring competition?

V. The **principals/owners** of the business and who will manage the business.

VI. **Employees** of the business (who, if known, how many, what salary you will pay, etc.).

VII. **Supplies** and other things you need to get started. This could include insurance, equipment, licenses and the like.

VIII. Identify and assess your **competition**. How will you fill the niches they've neglected and gain a competitive edge? How will you appeal to your target customers?

IX. How will you approach **marketing** your products and services? Catalogs? Telemarketing? Direct mail? Radio and T.V.? Who will be your sales force? As a rule, businesses invest a minimum 10% of yearly sales on marketing.

X. Who is your **target customer** and why would he/she want to buy your products or services? What age, gender, ethnicity, income group do you intend to reach? Be specific.

XI. What your **expected sales** will be the first year and how you came to that figure.

XII. How you will prepare for **growth**.

XIII. **Banks and investors** you plan to approach for money, when you plan to approach and how much you will request.

XIV. Where your **start-up capital** is coming from, when you expect to break even and when you expect to make a profit. Be sure to indicate exactly how you arrive at these figures.

XV. **Potential risks**. What will you do in the event of illness, breakdown of equipment, fire, theft, flood, etc.? What types of things could possibly go wrong and what will you do in each case? Think this through carefully.

XVI. **Exit strategy**. Circumstances may force you to close, sell or otherwise dissolve your business. An exit strategy is an integral part of your outline and business plan. Ask yourself: what costs and procedures can I expect to incur should I end my involvement in this venture?

As you work on your business outline, you'll keep thinking of things to add until you have several pages and probably discover the outline requires regular updating. When you feel you're ready to put together a formal business plan, obtain professional help. There are a number of how-to books and software programs on the market, if you want to handle task yourself. A listing of some popular software programs follow. Before spending any money though, seek help from the Small Business Administration. The SBA has two helpful booklets to order: *How to Write a Business Plan* and *Financing for the Small Business*. Both booklets explain the process of putting together a business plan in detail. Contact the SBA: 1-800 ASK-SBA.

The Government Printing Office's *Subject Bibliography* lists available publications on business management: Government Printing Office, Superintendent of Documents Washington, DC 20402-9328.

Business Plan Software

Business Plan Pro by Palo Alto Software • **www.palo-alto.com** (800) 229-7526

Biz Plan Builder by JIAN (800) 346-5426

Business Head Start by Planet Corp. • **www.planet-corp.com** (508) 757-2840

Power Business Plans by The Learning Company (800) 227-5609 **www.learningco.com**

On Your Way!

So, you've decided to embark on your own business venture. Congratulations and good luck! In order to put the wheels in motion and begin generating income, you will probably need all or most of the supplies listed:

- **Business cards and letterhead** to advertise.
- **A voice mail box and/or answering service.**
- **A fax machine and/or modem.**
- **A computer with a laser printer.**
- **A good quality computer desk and chair.**
- **A separate phone line** dedicated to faxing/internet.
- **A space** in which to conduct your business.
- **An e-mail address and/or website.**
- **Bookkeeping software.**
- **A Business-to-Business Directory.**

You may also need other equipment such as file cabinets, a typewriter, photocopier and scanner. A smart move: buy your furniture used. Check your local business-to-business directory for companies which sell used office furniture and shop around. I recently purchased a solid-steel computer desk and heavy-duty chair with excellent back support for $150 total!

E-Commerce and The Web

Having an email address nowadays is as common as having a telephone. Many companies expect to contact and correspond with you by email and people will automatically ask for your email address when they meet you. Having an email address is not very expensive. In fact, some companies now offer free email to any and everyone who signs up. You need a computer, modem and internet access however, to receive the freebies.

If you're interested in setting up your own website, you can establish a web hosting account with a service provider for "**virtual web hosting**." You'll have your own web address (called a domain name or URL) such as *www.delilahpower.com* and people will be able to visit your site and learn all about your company. A virtual web hosting account with basic features is fairly inexpensive, less than fifty dollars a month.

Tip: If you're creative and patient, design the website yourself with web authoring software such as Microsoft Frontpage and Adobe Image Styler. Cost: $150-$200.

Accepting credit card orders through your web site is more complicated and expensive. For starters, you must be established as a credit card merchant. Check with your bank for more information on accepting credit cards for purchases. Some banks/companies require purchase or lease of special software to conduct sales online. Prices for the software vary, so shop around.

Be aware online merchants must abide by specific laws. The Mail or Telephone Merchandise Order Rule for example, requires merchants to ship orders within a certain amount of time after charging a credit card. You must also notify a customer if you cannot ship a product when promised and allow the customer to cancel the order, if desired. Check out the following websites to learn more:

www.ftc.gov The Federal Trade Commission's (FTC) website. Log on to learn about the FTC, consumer rights, etc.

www.consumerworld.org A public service website that offers tips, advice and other forms of help.

The Home Office

Opening a home office can be a perfectly legal way to run a company, provided you follow a few guidelines and comply with the law. For many entrepreneurs, this is the ideal way to begin. Start-up costs are minimal and tax benefits can be significant. Note: Many cities and municipalities tax home-based businesses. Some even inflict an annual equipment tax. Speak with an accountant about the tax laws in your state and city prior to setting up shop in your residence.

If you set up shop at home, choose a space that's clearly defined and set apart from your living quarters. This makes it easier to determine your tax deductions for a home office at the end of the year. Make sure family members respect your work space and use that space for work only. Suggestion: Learn about Feng Shui, the ancient Chinese art of geomancy, how to choose the right space and arrange furniture so that your success and harmony with your surroundings can be increased.

Up and Running...

Once your business is up and running, you'll need to maintain it properly. Here are some tips:

- Refer to your business plan for daily operations and update your business plan every few months.
- Keep accurate and current records of all business transactions.
- Enroll in courses, workshops and seminars to increase your skills and knowledge.
- Join trade associations and organizations related to your business.
- Seek advice regularly from competent individuals.
- Network with other small business owners.
- Back up all electronic data and store it in a safe place, preferably a data safe. A regular fire-proof safe protects papers, but not computer disks.

Preparing for Tax Time

There are many allowable deductions for the small business owner: the cost of office furniture and equipment, supplies, costs to maintain the office (cleaning), legal fees, advertising, phone and utility bills and anything else purchased, used or needed to run the business. You may also be entitled to a deduction for the home office itself.

You can deduct auto expenses when you legitimately use your car for business. Meals and Entertainment expenses are deductible, for business meetings over dinner and business functions. If you travel (for seminars, expos, universities, conventions) you can deduct airfare, hotel, car rental, tuition, meals and so on. You must keep accurate records of all expenditures in order to satisfy the IRS during an audit. If you're not sure an item or expense is deductible, retain a record and speak to your accountant. You can also contact the Internal Revenue Service directly for advice. **Internal Revenue Service: (800) 829-1040**

Get the Help you Need!

If you're a member of a union, find out if they have a legal plan. You can save a tremendous amount of time and money dealing with routine business matters and prevent legal questions from becoming legal issues. Some legal plans contain business riders with unlimited telephone consultations, document review, collection, incorporation, real estate and more. They usually have attorneys or affiliated law firms who offer discounted hourly rates and maximum fee schedules.

Legal plans usually monitor and screen their participating attorneys to ensure you receive fair treatment and lessen your chances of encountering an unethical, unscrupulous lawyer. Many trade organizations also have legal plans as well as other benefits. Before joining a trade organization related to your field, look into the benefits offered. Spending a hundred dollars for a membership may save you thousands in the future.

Get the Money!

At some time during your business venture you will probably need to secure financing, borrow money, apply for credit or otherwise bankroll your endeavors. Some people create a company with the intention of selling it later, for a large profit. Whatever your goal, keep your company organized with meticulous records. When you approach a bank or individual investor, apply for a grant or otherwise look for funding, you can show where money is needed in your company, how the money will produce growth and most importantly, how you will repay the debt. The Small Business Administration can help you apply for loans and prepare a comprehensive business plan with a marketing strategy.

I've obtained information regarding several federally-funded programs for small businesses and would like to share that information with you. Contact them and say: "Show me the money!" Also listed are a number of web addresses you might want to investigate.

Small Business Administration (SBA) Programs

Women's Business Ownership Assistance: Contact the SBA, Office of Women's Business Ownership (202) 205-6673.

7(a)/11 Small Business Loans: For small businesses in areas of unemployment, business owners who are economically or socially disadvantaged. Contact the SBA, Loan Policy and Procedures Branch (202) 205-6570. **SBA:** 409 3rd Street, Washington, DC 20416.

Department of Commerce

Minority Business Development Centers: Grants provide business development to individuals and minorities. contact: Acting Deputy Director, Minority Business Development Agency, (202) 482-3237.

Department of Commerce: 14th and Constitution Ave. NW, Washington, DC 20230.

Department of Housing and Urban Development

Mortgage Insurance for individuals. Contact: Office of Business Products, (202) 708-2556/(202) 708-1422.

Youth-Youthbuild Programs: Public and non-profit organizations are both eligible. Contact: the Office of Economic Development at: (202) 708-2035.

Dept. of Housing and Urban Development: 451 SW 7th St., Washington, DC 20410.

Department of Agriculture

Business and Industrial Loans: Contact: Administrator, Rural Business Cooperative Service, (202) 690-4730/4737.

Department of Agriculture: 1440 SW Independence Ave. Washington, DC 20250

National Endowment for the Arts (NEA)

Promotion of the Arts and Grants to Organizations and Individuals. Contact: Deputy Chairman for Grants and Partnership, NEA (202) 682-5441/(202) 682-5400

NEA/NEH: 1100 Pennsylvania Avenue, NW Washington, DC 20506

National Endowment for the Humanities (NEH)

Fellowships and Stipends: Contact: Fellowships and Stipends office, Division of Research and Education, NEH (202) 606-8466.

Promotion of the Humanities: Funding and grants for projects which promote the humanities. Contact: Division of Preservation and Access, (202) 606-8570 / (202) 606-8309.

Bureau of Educational and Cultural Affairs (USIA)

Creative Arts Grants. Contact: Creative Arts Exchanges Program, Office of Citizen Exchanges, 301 4th St. SW Washington, DC 20547 (202) 205-2209

Institute of International Education

Cultural Exchange. Grants to promote U. S. participation in international festivals. Contact: Fund for U.S. Artists, Arts It'l, IIE, 809 United Nations Plaza, NYC 10017 (212) 883-8200.

Funding Sources and Information

www.businessfinance.com is a business capital search engine (America's Business Funding Directory). Locate venture capital for your business, commercial finance, equipment leasing, real estate, government programs and more.

www.fedmarket.com (Federal Marketplace) Search for government contracts, peruse the vendor directory, FedBuzz and Bids Weekly.

www.census.gov (U.S. Census Bureau) Access to the Census Bureau's most popular databases. For a nominal subscription fee, obtain business profiles for an area, counties economic and demographic info and more. This site also contains data on jobs, related sites, news, etc. It may take time and patience to fully explore this site, but you will probably find it's worth it. You can also call: (800) 392-6975.

www.companysleuth.com (Company Sleuth) Free information on companies you do business with or invest in.

www.dialogweb.com Log into this site and use their services to access professional publications and search business databases. Not a free service.

www.djnr.com (Dow Jones Interactive) Access databases of proprietary information not available on the web. Expect to incur a cost for their services.

www.hoovers.com (Hoover's Online) At this site, you can research companies for a fee.

www.knowx.com At this site, you can search public records of businesses and individuals. Cost involved. Run background checks, locate people, research businesses, etc.

www.lexisnexis.com (Lexis-Nexis) Search professional databases and articles that are not open to the web. There will be cost involved.

www.yourco.com (Your Company magazine). Business Briefs, polls, archives of previously published articles and Answer Men, where you can receive advice on law, tax, finance and more.

www.1step.com If you have established a web presence with your own web site, you can use their services to register with the various search engines. Not a free service.

Books, Publications and Software

The Prentice Hall Small Business Survival Guide, Prentice Hall, New Jersey. ISBN:0-13-045329-3.

The Complete Book of Small Business Forms and Agreements by Gustav Berle. Prentice Hall. ISBN: 0-13-841123-9.

The Elements of Feng Shui by Man-Ho Kwok, Barnes & Noble.

Peachtree Accounting (800) 247-3224 **www.peachtree.com**

Small Business Insurance Resources

Insuring Your Business by Sean Mooney, published by III Press. Call: (800) 331-9146.

www.iix.com (The Insurance Information Exchange)

www.cigna.com (Cigna)

www.iii.org (Insurance Information Institute) The Insurance Information Institute offers free brochures on Business Insurance which can be downloaded from the website or received by mail. Send a self-addressed, stamped envelope to: Insurance Information Institute (III), 110 William Street, New York, NY 10038

By deciding to own a business, you've chosen to empower yourself in a special way. The knowledge, insight, training and experience you'll receive will benefit you throughout your lifetime. Be proud of what you've set out to accomplish.

Visualize yourself earning a million dollars and manage your company with ambition. Adopt first-rate business policies, stay abreast of current technology and trends, know your market and tailor your products to meet the needs of your customers. Most of all, conduct all transactions with propriety and chances are your business will prosper for years to come.

Quote of the day: IRS: "We've got what it takes to take what you've got."

Part four

Completion

When Everything You Cultivate
Comes to Fruition...

The Solitary Queen

Sometimes, to truly honor yourself and maintain your dignity, you have to deal with being alone or lonely for a while. Honoring yourself may mean passing a certain man over, or letting go of a man who's not good for you. Getting out of a relationship and being alone for a while can in fact, be very healthy. For the woman seeking growth, it's an optimum time to explore herself and find out who she is, think about what she really wants from life and her relationships, and discover how she can seek her own happiness in a positive and meaningful way.

Unfortunately, being alone can be difficult and even painful. We all need to be loved, to feel physically and emotionally connected to someone. We like to have sex and we need men to make love to us. For these reasons, it's easier for some women to be with men who make them unhappy rather than gamble on finding someone new. Other women put a small value ticket on dignity and settle for anything, even if it's demeaning. These women should know the cost of self-respect is high, but with it comes a most valuable reward.

If you've recently gotten out of a relationship or had your heart broken, you might want to withdraw from men altogether. This is a common reaction to being hurt and/or disappointed. Closing yourself down to withdraw temporarily is not unhealthy, unless you feel you can never open yourself again. The more you withdraw, the harder it may be to recognize when it's time to receive someone worthy. You must be receptive to love in order for it to find you. If your heartache is too severe to bear, you may need outside help in order to heal. For some women, a therapist, spiritual advisor or doctor may be the best remedy.

Just because you're alone, you don't have to be lonely. You can use your time constructively to take care of yourself and broaden your horizons, learn new things and do whatever you enjoy: socializing, hobbies, etc. You can also do something to change your appearance: buy some new clothes if you can afford it, improve your muscle tone with exercise and get a make-over so that you feel more attractive.

Recovering from Heartbreak

Recovering from heartbreak requires an aggressive approach on your part. Rather than focus on the man and how he hurt you, it may help you to focus solely on *yourself* and what you can do to heal. Put your efforts into what's best for you, without giving the man consideration. If you attempt to seek revenge in some way or evoke a particular sentiment from him, you are wasting valuable energy.

Channel your energies into moving on with your life. Release your regrets and forgive yourself for any mistakes you feel you've made. Keep reminding yourself that you are worthy of love and happiness. Look for a positive lesson in the experience, bless the past and release it. If one man doesn't perform well, you can be sure it's because someone better is waiting in the wings, ready to take the stage.

Back in the Saddle

Once the emotional healing process is underway, you can decide when it's time to reopen yourself and find someone new. To attract a new male, you'll have to take some social risks. While an all-out manhunt is time and energy consuming, you *should* get out and make yourself available to the right people in the right locations.

Many women who are lonely look for relationships in the wrong settings. Although bars and nightclubs tend to house lots of males, they're probably the worst places to search for men of substance. If you're just looking for sex, these spots may be for you. If you want more than a quick romp with a beautiful stranger, consider these alternatives: museums, community meetings, libraries, bookstores and churches.

Sometimes, a change of environment can produce great results. Consider what you're interested in and determine where men with the same interests can be found. Seek contact with men who have similar backgrounds: education, socioeconomic status and the like. Aim to develop friendships before establishing intimate relationships. A man you think isn't your type initially can turn out to be your best choice for love, marriage and fatherhood.

After being out of dating circles for a while, reestablishing a presence amongst your peers can feel rather awkward. If you're shy about meeting men, or feel your confidence has been shaken, work to bolster your social skills and conquer your fear of rejection. Practice flirting with men in whom you have no interest *first*, since there's little or nothing at stake. Once you've rebuilt your confidence, you'll interact more successfully with those men who really pique your curiosity.

The most effective way to attract men is to maintain a positive attitude and what's called a *joie de vivre* or, joy for living. Love of life will make you immensely attractive to the opposite sex. Someone once told me:

Of all the things you wear, your expression is the most important.

Heartache can transform a beautiful face into one that is hard and bitter. Be conscious of how your facial expressions may appear to others and smile frequently. A smile is a powerful love magnet. Smiling also lifts the spirit, balances the emotions and brightens the aura. Allow yourself to glow despite your pain. Although you can't choose every turn in the course of your life, you *can* choose to smile and make yourself feel happier.

Love Yourself. You are Queen!

Learn about yourself. Explore who you are and offer no explanations for how you feel. Find your own truths in life and look for a lesson in each experience. Don't try to be better than others, be the best that you can be. Find out what it is you want from life and go after it.

Validate yourself. Take pride in all accomplishments, big and small. Rather than criticize, learn to evaluate objectively. Be less judgmental of yourself and more patient with others. Push yourself to continually move forward, leaving negativity behind.

Take care of yourself. Body and mind united create a strong woman. Worship the body, develop the intellect and build yourself spiritually with prayer, self-reflection and meditation. Develop your own set of morals and stick by them. Live for yourself and not the expectations of others.

⊛ Confront and conquer your fears, remembering that *fear is only misuse of the imagination.*

⊛ Share yourself with others and give the gift of love.

⊛ Take time to appreciate the little things in life.

⊛ Surround yourself with cheerful, positive people, get rid of those who are negative.

⊛ Never let rejection deter you. Sometimes you have to wade through a sea of "no" in order to locate an island of "yes".

⊛ Make your birthday a personal holiday. Birthdays are New Year's day in disguise because they mark a new astrological cycle. Try making your resolutions on that day rather than at the beginning of a new calendar year.

Related Resource: *10 Bad choices that ruin black women's lives* by Dr. Grace Cornish, published by Crown.

Goddess of Love Pancakes ™
(with Blueberries)

If you want to please a man's palate (or your own), serve up these heavenly pancakes made from scratch. You will enjoy celestial bliss, he will kneel down and worship you!

1 cup all-purpose flour, sifted
2 tablespoons cornmeal
1 tablespoon sugar
1 tablespoon baking powder
½ teaspoon baking soda
¼ teaspoon salt
¼ teaspoon cinnamon
1 teaspoon vanilla extract
1 egg, beaten
1 cup buttermilk or vanilla yogurt
2 tablespoons vegetable oil
1 cup fresh blueberries, washed thoroughly
confectioners sugar (if desired)

Combine flour, cornmeal, sugar, baking powder, baking soda, salt and cinnamon in a bowl. Set the dry mixture aside. In a medium sized bowl, combine the egg, buttermilk, oil and vanilla. Add the wet mixture to the dry and stir until fully moistened. Do not over mix, batter should be slightly lumpy. Next, gently fold in the blueberries.

Preheat and lightly grease your griddle or pan. Pour out pancakes until about 4 inches in diameter. Cook pancakes until surface is bubbly and edges are dry before turning. This should take about 2 minutes. Only turn pancakes once.

Pancakes are done when golden brown. Serve hot with butter, syrup, whipped cream and/or powdered sugar, jam or blueberry sauce. Some health-conscious goddesses enjoy their pancakes topped with plain or vanilla yogurt.
Rating: ☆☆☆

Nefertiti's Nookie Cookies ™

Queen Nefertiti of Egypt was known for her incredible beauty and romantic allure. These sensuous cookies unite love with the sands of time. Serve Nookie Cookies for breakfast with Ceylon black tea or before bed with a quality fruit liqueur. As the name suggests, Nookie Cookies taste great after a naughty episode.

½ cup pecans, chopped
½ cup softened butter
1 cup self-rising flour
¼ cup confectioners sugar
¼ cup brown sugar
½ teaspoon vanilla
¼ teaspoon cinnamon
¼ teaspoon nutmeg
confectioners sugar (sifted) to dust cookies after baked
ungreased cookie sheet

Using a large fork, mix pecans, butter, flour, sugar, vanilla, cinnamon and nutmeg in a medium-sized bowl. Spoon a tablespoon of dough into hands and roll. Place on ungreased cookie sheet and curve into crescent shape. Make sure cookies are spaced at least an inch apart. Bake at 375 degrees for about 12 minutes. Cookies should be set, but not browned. Roll Nookie Cookies in sifted confectioners sugar immediately after baking and sprinkle again before serving. Makes about 18 cookies.

For a tasty variation, try using crushed almonds in lieu of pecans. In addition to vanilla, add almond extract and a teaspoon of honey. Serve in your bedroom palace with all the amenities. Make him your sexual slave: tell him to get on his knees and service you because you're royalty.   Rating: ☆☆☆

Intimate Connections

Connecting intimately with a man means much more than having sex with him. When there's no emotional involvement, sex can in fact, be rather *impersonal*. Some women like impersonal sex and have the right as consenting adults. If however you want to connect with a man on a deep spiritual and emotional level, you need to approach him with an intimate connection in mind.

What Exactly is an Intimate Connection?

An intimate connection is a special kind of relationship that provides both people with sincere and lasting contentment. You can be married, engaged, committed, involved, single or just having fun. Whatever might be your situation, you genuinely care for (or love) the man, have an understanding and feel comfortable with him. Even if you're not committed to one another, you both have a commitment to *honesty*. Honesty inspires trust and trust inspires emotion. An intimate connection is healthy because it encourages personal *growth*.

Setting the stage for an Intimate connection

Unfortunately, some men are incapable of having real intimate connections with women due to character flaws, lack of maturity and/or emotional issues. At the same time, some women say they want intimacy, but sabotage their own efforts to obtain it. To set the stage for an intimate connection, you have to be ready for intimacy *yourself*. Since intimate connections require a mature outlook, the man you intend to partner with must be chosen with care. You'll know you've made a solid choice when you can complete the following check-list after getting to know a man:

My New Male Friend...

- ☐ is positive, productive and ambitious.
- ☐ appears committed to personal growth.
- ☐ is willing to learn.
- ☐ has integrity.
- ☐ is selective about the women he dates.
- ☐ shows emotional openness.
- ☐ can teach me something valuable about life.
- ☐ accepts me as I am and allows me to be myself.
- ☐ inspires me to be more productive and creative.
- ☐ respects my own personal space.
- ☐ offers his honesty in return for my own.
- ☐ wants what I want from a relationship.
- ☐ protects himself and others by practicing safe sex.

If you cannot complete this checklist and/or are unhappy with your past and present relationships, it may be time for you to look closely at:

❧ **The choices you're making**. You are in complete control of your relationships and have the power to *choose* what you want. If you are in an unhealthy situation, choose to get out of it. In the future, choose men who can offer you what you need.

❧ **The judgments you formulate about the men you meet**. Some females pass negative judgments on Black men who don't deserve them. A hard-working Brother with a low-paying, honest job for example, has far more character and reason for self-pride than a hood-rat who plunders his community by selling drugs and engaging in crime. If material gain at any cost is your motto, then a thug may be your man. But, don't expect decent treatment from him.

There was a woman who found an injured cobra. Feeling sorry for the animal, she wrapped it gingerly in a blanket and took it home. For several days she nursed the snake and began to care for it so much, she decided to keep it as a pet. Eventually, the snake regained its full health. Then one day while cleaning the cobra's cage, the woman reached out to touch the snake and it bit her.

"How could you do this?" she cried, dying, "After all I've done for you, how could you betray me this way?"

"It was easy," the snake hissed, "But then, you knew I was a snake when you took me in."

Some men (such as drug dealers), are easily recognizable serpents. Other men cover their true natures with a false skin they eventually shed. If you meet a snake and still choose to bring it into your life, close to your heart, don't be surprised when it bites you. A snake is poisonous and will always act according to its nature. If you forget you're dealing with a snake, or expect a snake to change its nature, you've made a fatal error in judgment.

❦ **The way you feel about yourself**. Loving yourself means taking care of yourself, refusing to accept less than a man's best. Love can't thrive when fear and insecurity are present. If you're not secure and happy within yourself, you won't find happiness in a relationship. Instead of looking for a man, try looking within. Take some time to find yourself and explore ways to release your fears and insecurities.

❦ **The manner in which you deal with the men you meet**. Are you sabotaging your ability to find true love? Some women have commitment anxiety and either run from men who can offer them stability, or select men who are already involved with someone, emotionally shut down, or otherwise unavailable. If you have commitment anxiety and are unhappy about it, you may need the help of a therapist to get to the root of your issues.

Investing in Love:
A "Get Rich Quick" Scheme for the Heart

If you've ever observed how men tend to approach their relationships, they seem to do so with more detachment than women. While we're reading romance novels, fantasizing and searching for "the perfect man", men are selecting certain women for relationships because they feel these women will make good wives or mothers. For some men, logic overrides emotion and unrequited love becomes the last consideration in a relationship or marriage. Perhaps this is why so many of them can cheat without guilt.

Unless you're very wealthy, you probably count your nickels and keep close track of your dollars. You budget yourself from paycheck to paycheck, look for bargains and try to spend wisely. In the end, you manage because you play it smart. The suggestion now is that you apply basic financial principles to your relationships. If you approach relationships the way you approach managing your money, scrutinize the men you meet and take care when spending your emotions, you'll end up with someone who can give you a large return. You'll get rich quick and enjoy emotional wealth.

- **Carefully evaluate a prospect before you invest.** Would you throw money away on a get-rich scheme that appears to be a scam? Why then, would you invest emotions in someone who seems shady?

- **Diversify your investments.** In other words, don't put all your energy and emotion into one man until and unless he proves he's worth it. Spread your attention around and enjoy the variety. Socialize, date and leave yourself open to new experiences, even *after* you're involved. You can maintain an honest commitment and still keep your eyes open.

❦ **You should show your portfolio only to those that are qualified**. Your past is your own personal business. You are not required to tell a man all of your intimate secrets. In fact, it may be unwise to do so. The more you trust a man, the more you can tell him. However, some things should always be kept to yourself, in the closet.

❦ **Avoid investments that are "projects"**. Projects are men with emotional problems, drug problems and other serious problems. Forget about trying to "fix" men with problems. Like experiments, men who are projects tend to be very unpredictable. Unless you have a strong science background and know how to mix combustible chemicals, your "project" might blow up in your face.

❦ **Decide how much you should invest**. If you meet a man who's obviously about game, why put your heart in it? The likelihood is, you'll be disappointed.

❦ **Never invest more in a prospect than you can afford to lose**. Remember, a game can have only one winner. If you're a player, know the rules and play to win. At the same time, prepare to count your losses. If and when you do lose, it's easier to move on.

❦ **If your losses begin to exceed your gains, pull out**. A relationship should be profitable for you emotionally and in other ways. If the cons keep outweighing the pros, or if you continue to take a loss, you'll eventually end up dead broke: mentally, physically and spiritually.

❦ **Keep your eyes open in case you come across a more profitable investment**. Smart investors watch the market and constantly reassess the value of their stock. This isn't cheating, this is sound financial principle. The higher your stock's value, the tighter you should hold onto it.

An Option is an Option...

Men come in all shapes, sizes and colors. With so many to choose from, why limit yourself to dating only one type? There are men from every ethnic group who can make marvelous husbands, lovers and companions. If a man treats you well, it shouldn't matter where he comes from or what he looks like. When it comes to men, all that glitters is *not* gold and gold is often found in the most *unlikely* places. If you're searching for a romantic treasure, leave no stone unturned. Expand your dating circle to include what you'd normally consider the unconventional.

Do You Take this Man...

Marriage can be a wonderful joining of two people. There are a number of books on the market which give advice on how to get a man to marry you, many women swear by them. While marriage is a life-long goal for some women, others are not so anxious to tie the knot. If you want a man to marry you, determine whether the man is really *worth* marrying before pursuing him.

Some women make the grave mistake of coercing a man into marrying them, or marrying a man out of desperation. Family pressures, cultural background and age can also influence a woman's desire to find a husband. Since marriage is not a cure-all solution to personal problems or relationship issues, some women get married and still find themselves unhappy.

If you're seeking a husband, remember a marriage is more than a love union, it is a *binding contract*. In order for a marriage to work, both parties must be willing to work constantly on the relationship. What you see is what you get. If the man you love has fidelity issues or other serious problems, marrying him won't necessarily change his behavior. You have a better chance at success however, if you seek professional counseling prior to walking down the isle.

Love without sensibility is often blind. If your man is unfaithful, don't let him blame his actions on his physiology, temptation, another woman, or you. It's about a *choice* he makes and he knows exactly what he's doing.

The Carrot Method

What is "The Carrot Method" and how can it work for you? The Carrot Method is an effective way of dealing with an unruly, stubborn man. Its principles are based on a tried-and-true method of training obstinate horses. The Carrot Method works because it motivates a man to behave without his feeling controlled or resentful.

When dealing with a stubborn horse, trainers use a carrot to entice the animal into submission: the carrot is placed on a stick just beyond the horse's reach, encouraging the animal to move forward so that he can eat it. Since the horse never reaches the carrot, he'll continue to advance until halted by the trainer.

When using The Carrot Method on a man, you'll approach handling his behavior in two separate ways:

- You will encourage him with kindness rather than correct him with anger.

- You will give him sight of a prize for which he must constantly reach.

Encourage him with kindness. As the expression goes, speak softly and carry a big stick. When your man displeases you, allow a cool-out time for yourself before approaching him. Attempt to reason with him before resorting to other measures. Express your concerns gently and be firm about what you want. Kindness is weakness only when in absence of common sense.

When your man becomes unruly, instead of nagging him, entice him. Be nice, be sweet and *be unavailable*. If you live together, find reasons to stay out of the house more, making sure you look your best when he sees you leave. If you're dating a man who's beginning to take you for granted, upset his game plan. When he calls you, be nice, be sweet, but *be unavailable*. Put him off in a way that says; "I'll make myself available to you again when you're ready to treat me correctly."

Give him sight of the prize. Make happiness the prize and make him reach. Remind a man with positive actions he has much to gain by having you as his woman. Keep yourself tight at all times: looking good, smelling good and feeling good. A righteous man is worth the work, so long as he's willing to work for you. Need him without being needy. When you're down, expect him to be to support you. Share problems with your man, taking care not to become problematic.

Once you have an intimate connection with a man, make it strong, make it solid and make it last!

❦ If you want respect, give it to get it and keep it!

❦ Remember love is like a bank account: you can't withdraw on it unless you make deposits.

❦ Accept that men don't always communicate in the same way as women. Approach a man to talk when he's most receptive. Most men will tell you when they're in the mood to talk, if you ask.

❦ Switch roles with your partner occasionally and take on the responsibilities of the other. This can help you to develop empathy and understand each other's perceptions.

❦ Let a man be a man (whatever *that* means). Sometimes men feel a need to do "male" things, like hang out with the boys, whoop, yell and holler at a game, belch, fart and act disgusting with a beer in their hands, rebel against the establishment, etc. (Hard to understand, but you get the picture).

❦ Give a man his space and he'll always come back to you. A man in love will live up to your expectations if you trust him.

"Sometimes, it's okay to wake up grumpy; other times, just let him sleep."

❧ Support your man and remember he's changing and growing each day, just as you are. Allow him to grow and don't be threatened by positive change.

❧ Establish whether the man is merely involved or totally committed. The difference between real involvement and commitment can be related to ham and eggs: with ham and eggs, the chicken is involved but the pig is *committed*. When a man makes a decision to be committed, he puts an integral part of himself into the relationship.

❧ Last but not least, show him you care every chance you get and he'll do the same.

Are You Being Abused?

If you're with a man who causes you any kind of pain and suffering (physical, mental, emotional), you may be in an abusive relationship. Abuse is not limited to his hitting or beating you, abuse can take many forms. If your man constantly criticizes and demeans you, threatens you (or people close to you) and makes you fear him, destroys personal property, withholds money, controls your finances and/or forces you to have sex with him, he is abusive. He is also dangerous and will continue the abuse unless you do what's necessary to stop him.

Love is no reason to endure abuse, nor is love a reason to put your life in danger. Domestic/relationship abuse is a serious problem for which you are not to blame. You do need to get help. NOW!

National Organization for Victim Assistance (NOVA)
1757 Park Road NW, Washington, DC 20010
(800) TRY-NOVA (202) 232-6682 www.access.digcx.net/~nova

National Victims Resource Center
Box 6000, Rockville, MD 20849 (800) 627-6872 www.ncjrs.org

International Child Abduction/Adoption: (202) 736-7000

Partnership to Prevent Domestic Violence
Victim Services: (800) 621-HOPE/(212) 874-8526
Children's Defense Fund: (202) 628-8787

www.serve.com/zone (The safety Zone) A website for victims of domestic violence. Ways to find help and support.

www.dvsheltertour.org (Victim Services: Domestic Violence Shelter Tour) Information on abuse and how to prevent or escape it. A map lists help organizations in every state.

www.chebucto.ns.ca (Chebucto Community Net) Men for Change and other features.

If you are the victim of a domestic crime, you may be eligible for benefits from your state's Crime Victim Compensation Board. Benefits could include expenses for medical and other related services not covered by other insurance or benefit programs, lost earnings or loss of support, burial expenses, occupational re-habilitation expenses, counseling expenses and the cost of repair or replacement of essential personal property lost as a result of a crime.

To obtain these benefits, contact the Crime Victim Compensation Board in your state. To locate the Crime Victim Compensation Board in your area, call the National Association of Crime Victim Compensation Boards below or the Office for Victims of Crime.

National Association of Crime Victim Compensation Boards
P.O. Box 16003, Alexandria, VA 22302 (703) 370-2996

Office for Victims of Crime/U.S. Dept. of Justice: (202) 307-5983

Relationship abuse affects women from all walks of life, so you are not alone. Don't let fear of a man's wrath paralyze you. Talk about your problems with someone you respect and trust, protect yourself by contacting the organizations listed previously and get away from him. You deserve to be safe, well and happy.

Black, Proud, Aware!

Being a Black woman is something to be very proud of. You have incredible genes, a unique heritage and an abundance of talents passed on to you by mighty ancestors. Your Nubian beauty (rich skin, full lips and voluptuous body) is unsurpassed and imitated by women the world over. God has given you a wonderful gift and it is up to you to make the most of it. Stand tall and deliver!

Unfortunately, many of us say we're proud to be Black or African-American, but act otherwise. The truth is, many of us feel no real connection to Africa, but pretend we do out of a sense of obligation. Furthermore, we've been so conditioned to dislike ourselves as a people, some of us keep passing the curse of self-hatred on in a vicious cycle from generation to generation. Misery loves company, as they say. In order for us to advance, the cycle of self-hatred has to end. *You* have the power to determine when and how. You *can* make a difference.

Changing the way you think is not an easy process, especially when you've been raised to have a certain mentality or negatively conditioned by your experiences. For example, no person of color should avoid the sun to prevent getting any "blacker", or think someone with long, straight hair has "good hair". Thoughts like these stem from a history of brainwashing by Europeans. If you've been "psyched out", you don't have to stay that way. You can look within, find the truth and choose to be proud of what you are: Black, and beautiful!

Dealing with Racism

Racism is something every Black person experiences at some time or another. Whenever it happens, you feel a degree of confusion and hurt. Racism is difficult to understand because it has no justifiable or logical basis. Contrary to what some people say however, you *don't* have to live with racism. It can surround your space yet not enter. It can exist in other people's consciousness and never affect yours. In other words, racism is something you can live *without*.

Racists are fearful bullies who have nothing to offer the world except hatred. They cover their uselessness with delusions of superiority and they lack spirituality. When racists attempt to insult, demean and hurt you, it's not because something's wrong with you, it's because something's wrong with *them*. The only way they can define themselves is to destroy others. Some are vicious enough to resort to violence and murder.

Most frightening are the white supremacists who, as you read this, are waging what they call a "Racial Holy War" against people of color in this country. According to an article in *U.S. News & World Report* (July 19, 1999), there were over 500 hate groups operating in the U.S. in 1998 and their numbers are steadily increasing. These groups are using First Amendment protections and the internet to spread their hateful views and recruit new members. They're also arming themselves with weapons. Hate crimes are on the rise. Every person of color should consider this cause for alarm and take steps to protect themselves and their families.

Our best defense against a growing climate of hatred is to stick together: communicate, convey information and utilize all resources. Make your voice heard by voting and know what's going on in our government. Don't let dangerous people make their problems your own. Keep your eyes open and stay informed. Be aware of what's going on around you and use common sense to protect yourself and your loved ones from harm.

If and when you experience racism, especially when spending money, don't feed into it. Refuse to accept it. Work to control your anger and keep your cool. Use your head. Remember what we talked about in *Money Madness*. Black people in America represent billions of dollars in spending power. Exercise that power. Spend your valuable dollars where they will most benefit you and other people of color!

Increasing Awareness

The person who believes ignorance is bliss is indeed the fool. Increase your awareness by finding out as much as you can about the world around you. Here are just a few ways to free your mind:

- Open yourself to new experiences. Be willing to try new and unusual things (foods, activities, etc).
- Forget about stereotypes. Learn more about people of other races and cultures.
- Talk to people you meet. Listen to their ideas and try to understand their perspectives.
- Read news magazines such as U.S. News and World Report, Emerge and Black Enterprise.
- Use the information superhighway (internet) to seek out and gather information.
- Most important of all, learn more about *yourself*. Read about Black history and the many important contributions we've made to this world, A listing of informative books on Black accomplishments and inventors follows at the end of this section.

As we've said all along, knowledge is power and power can take you everywhere. So, the more you know, the farther you'll go!

Unfortunately, we as African-Americans do not maximize our spending power. Instead of internalizing our resources and pooling together, we tend to spend our dollars in places which benefit the vendors and not the community. Before we can see solid growth as a people, we must unify financially.

Businesses that set up shop in Black communities without improving the community's conditions do not deserve your dollars, nor do foreign vendors who come to this country barely speaking English, have no respect for Black people and open stores in Black communities to improve life for themselves and their own people elsewhere. These types of businesses are raping us financially. So, each time you spend a dollar, think about where that dollar is going. Most importantly, patronize Black-owned businesses whenever possible.

Another consideration: whenever you pay for media which perpetuates negative stereotypes of Black people (movies, novels, etc.), you *promote* those stereotypes. If a film, book or any other media offends and insults you, show your strength. Protest by writing to the source. More importantly, use your spending power. Boycott.

Making Strides

The **National Council of Negro Women**, Inc. (NCNW) is a nonprofit membership organization founded by Mary McLeod Bethune. NCNW sponsors women's and girl's leadership training, health improvement, economic empowerment and international development. Benefit plans include Medicare supplement, Cancer Protector Insurance Plan, dental, automobile and homeowners insurance. Annual membership is $25. (800) 808-4514, (800) 808-4517, or (202) 737-0120. NCNW also accepts contributions. Contributions are tax deductible.

African-American Genealogy

Knowledge of where you come from can help you to understand and clearly define who you are. Genealogy is the act of documenting your family tree. Through research, you can trace your bloodlines as far back in time as possible, to a common set of ancestors. Imagine the amazing stories and wealth of information you can uncover! Genealogy forms the basis of family history. If you were to picture a great and powerful tree, genealogy is the trunk that supports the events (limbs) and experiences (leaves) of your entire family.

Knowing your family's history can help to make your family stronger. Many of us have no idea who our real ancestors are. We acknowledge our African roots, but can we say exactly where in Africa these roots are buried? What about those of us with Native-American heritage? Researching your family history can give you a new perspective on life and yourself, as well as a feeling of security and a positive identity.

Just so you understand the task at hand, genealogy involves extensive research. The results however, will be immensely rewarding. If you're really interested in documenting your family tree, you might want to join a local genealogy society for assistance and guidance. To locate a genealogy society in your area, contact the National Afro-American Historical Genealogical Society in Washington DC at: (202) 234- 5350.

Related Resources

Africana, Kwame Anthony Appiah and Henry Louis Gates, Jr., editors. A one volume encyclopedia offering an entire history of Africa and the African Diaspora. Basic Civitas Books.

American Legacy: Celebrating African-American History and Culture. A quarterly magazine. Direct subscription inquiries to: AMERICAN LEGACY, Subscription Office, P.O. Box 5441, Harlan, IA 51593. Call 800-454-4997.

Black Stars African-American Inventors by Otha Richard Sullivan, John Wiley & Sons.

Facts About Blacks by Raymond M. Corbin, published by Madison Books. ISBN: 1-56833-081-2.

Famous Firsts of Black Americans by Sibyl Hancock, Pelican Publishing Company. ISBN: 0-88289240-1.

Great African-American Women by Darryl Lyman, published by Jonathan David Publishers. ISBN: 0-8246-0142-1.

Privacy Rules

Privacy is something you must fight to protect at all times. Many people don't concern themselves with privacy issues until it's too late. Unfortunately, privacy is like innocence: once lost, it's gone forever. In today's information age, it's fairly easy for other people to learn intimate details about you and use the information for unscrupulous purposes.

For example, someone with criminal savvy who also knows your social security number can open fraudulent accounts in your name and even get their hands on your savings. Others can take unethical peeks into your personal life without your knowledge. The questions is, just how much do you want others to know about you?

Whenever you use charge cards, store credit cards, club cards and discount cards, companies compile personal data about you by tracking your purchases. Many include printed surveys with warranty information for their products in order to learn more about your habits and lifestyle and ask personal questions you are not required by law to answer. As a general rule, I don't complete these surveys nor do I recommend you do so either. Purchase very personal items with cash and limit the information you give to any merchant.

"Your call may be monitored and/or recorded to ensure quality service."

Chances are you've heard a recorded message to this effect when calling businesses. It happens so routinely, you might ignore it or assume companies are exercising a legal right. The fact is, you may be able to refuse having your calls monitored and recorded.

The **Federal Communications Commission** (FCC) protects the privacy of interstate phone conversations by requiring the other party to notify you and seek your verbal or written consent before recording you. If you don't object to being recorded, you've relinquished your right to a particular form of privacy.

Each state has its own **Public Service Commission** which may also protect you. If you don't like the idea of parties listening to and recording your conversations, do something about it. The Public Service Commission should be listed in the government section of your phone directory. To contact the FCC: (888) 225-5322.

Protect yourself against fraud. Don't give your social security number (SSAN) to anyone unless absolutely necessary. Many companies ask for SSANs even though they're not legally entitled to it. Never give your SSAN to make a purchase (such as books or music from a club), or utilize a common service (such as joining a local gym). When you show I.D., make sure it doesn't reveal your SSAN. Carry the minimum amount of I.D. and cards which contain your SSAN.

Never leave a banking receipt at an ATM location, you give others easy access to your bank accounts and your money.

Know your mail pattern. Carefully review your bills as soon as they arrive and never leave outgoing mail in an unsecured mailbox. Take mail to the post office or drop it in an official postal box.

Never complete surveys over the phone and don't give out personal information over the phone unless you've initiated the call. Avoid discussing personal and intimate issues over the phone and placing credit card orders with a cordless phone.

Avoid paper trails. Whatever you put in writing or sign your name to can follow you around the rest of your life. Also, e-mail is forever and can be sent all over the world. In short, some things are better left unrecorded.

Invest in a paper shredder and thoroughly shred every personal document you throw away. There are some people who spend their time digging through garbage cans in search of banking information, social security numbers and credit card information.

Knowledge is Power!

No one can stop you when you know where you've come from and where you're going. No one can deter you when your vision and focus are clear. We are borne from a legacy of brilliant and resourceful people. It is a blessing to be Black. Stay proud and stay aware!

Internet Intelligence Service: EWATCH: **www.ewatch.com**
ECLIPZE: **www.eclipze.com**

Black Interest Web Sites

www.bigblackbook.com (Big Black Book) Black business directory. Soul Exchange, Afro-American Web Ring and more.

www.netnoir.com (The Black Network) An online store geared for the Black community. Buy Black products by Black people. Includes education, Netnoir, chathouse, Black Boards, free email, Black Web, newsletter and more.

www.socialstep.com   (Social Step)   Includes Business, Travel, Social Scene, Cultural Horizon and more.

www.soulsearch.net   (Soul Search)   A Black search engine with links to a number of Black web sites. If you have your own web site, register with them.

www.what2read.com African-American online bookstore. Source of Black literature, booklists, what's new, discussions and web chat.

Quote of the day: "Always remember you're unique, just like everyone else."

The Last Page of my Personal Chapter

This is the final page you'll write in this book, but your success is just beginning! Some final thoughts: Where am I, now that I've finished reading this book? How has it helped me? What are my expectations for improvement in my life and how will I make positive change?

_____

_____

_____

_____

_____

_____

_____

_____

_____

_____

_____

_____

_____

Best of luck and many blessings. Write on! ✎ *More space on reverse...*

Index

About the Author

Tannis Blackman is a certified Dance instructor and health and fitness enthusiast. Deeply spiritual and devoted to personal growth, she has always been fascinated by "New Age" topics and holistic healing. Tannis has spent years gathering unique and useful information for her first book entitled, Delilah Power! She currently teaches Dance and fitness in New York City and is studying Tarot interpretation under renowned Tarot Master Chuck Wagner.

Her second book entitled, The Mystical Seductress Handbook, is a popular manual which offers a New Age approach to love in the next millennium.

Future plans include travel to Egypt, where she intends to further research Tarot divination. Although the Tarot's imagery and meaning have been obscured by Europeans in recent centuries, it's appearance in ancient Egyptian hieroglyphics indicates it is of African origin. Tannis hopes to produce a new deck much like the original created in Egypt and thus help to preserve our incredible history.

Chuck Wagner: Tarot Master and Astrologer
4 Park Avenue, New York, NY 10016 • (212) 725-8849
Private Sessions or by Mail

Bibliography

American Red Cross. *Community First Aid & Safety*. St. Louis, MO: 1993.

Blackman, Tannis. *The Mystical Seductress Handbook*. New York: Swing Street Publishing, 2000.

Cannon, Angie, and Warren Cohen. *"The Church of the Almighty White Man."* U.S. News & World Report, 19 July, 1999, pp. 22-24.

Cosmopolitan Books. *Cosmopolitan's Guide to Fortune-Telling*. New York: 1974.

Fisher, Helen. *Anatomy of Love, The Natural History of Monogamy, Adultery, and Divorce*. New York: W.W.Norton and Company, 1992.

Flodin, Kim. *"African-American Healthcare: Strategies for the New Millennium."* American Legacy, Fall, 1999, pp. 1-8.

Gordon, Barry. *Memory, Remembering and Forgetting in Everyday Life*. New York: Mastermedia Limited, 1995.

Morris, Desmond, Peter Collett, Peter Marsh, and Marie O'shaughnessy. *Gestures, their origins and distribution*. New York: Stein and Day, 1979.

Moyers, Bill. *Healing and The Mind*. New York: Doubleday, 1993.

Pickering, David. *Dictionary of Superstitions*. London: Cassel, 1995.

Righteous Mother, The. *Sex Her Right! A Brother's Guide to the Most Intimate Details*. New York: Swing Street Publishing, 1999.

Righteous Mother, The. *Get on Top! A Sister's Guide to Life, Love and her Biggest Difficulty...* Second Ed. New York: Swing Street Publishing, 1999.

Taber, Clarence W. *Taber's Cyclopedic Medical Dictionary*. New York: F.A. Davis Company, 1970.

Tannahill, Reay. *Sex in History*. New York: Stein & Day, 1980.

Order Form

Call **Toll Free: 1 (888) GO-GIRL 1**. 1 (888) 464-4751. AMEX, VISA
and MasterCard accepted.

Postal Orders: Swing Street Publishing, P.O. Box 846, Cathedral Station,
New York 10025-0846. Tel: (212) 969-8122. Send Check or money order
payable to: Swing Street. Visit our website at: www.goswingstreet.com

Please send the following books:

<u>Cost:</u>

_____

_____

_____

New York residents must add 8 1/4 sales tax. **Sales Tax:** _____
Allow 2-4 weeks delivery. Include S&H.
Shipping: $3.00 first book, $1.00 each additional.

Shipping: _____

Total: _____

Payment (circle one): Check /Money order Major credit card

Type of credit card: _____

Name appearing on card: _____

Card number: _____

Expiration date: _____/ _____

Cardholder's Signature: _____

Mailing Address: _____

_____

_____

Order Form

Call **Toll Free: 1 (888) GO-GIRL 1**. 1 (888) 464-4751. AMEX, VISA and MasterCard accepted.

Postal Orders: Swing Street Publishing, P.O. Box 846, Cathedral Station, New York 10025-0846. Tel: (212) 969-8122. Send Check or money order payable to: Swing Street. Visit our website at: www.goswingstreet.com

Please send the following books:

<u>**Cost:**</u>

_____

_____

_____

New York residents must add 8 1/4 sales tax.   **Sales Tax:**   _____
Allow 2-4 weeks delivery. Include S&H.
Shipping: $3.00 first book, $1.00 each additional.

Shipping: _____

Total: _____

Payment (circle one): Check /Money order   Major credit card

Type of credit card: _____

Name appearing on card: _____

Card number: _____

Expiration date: _____/ _____

Cardholder's Signature: _____

Mailing Address: _____

_____

_____